PRAISE FROM SALES TH
AND ELITE TR/

The #1 reason for failure in sales is an empty pipeline. And the #1 reason your pipeline is empty is that you avoid cold calling. In this book, Armand & Nick inspire you to get past your mental hangups, pick up the phone, and start cold calling. **Read it now. Your bank account will thank you!**

—Jeb Blount,
Bestselling Author of *Fanatical Prospecting*

At the surface, objections like "not interested" or "taken care of" appear to reject whatever we're trying to sell. But the reality is that a prospect is often resisting the mere thought of change, or the interruption of the cold call itself. In *Cold Calling Sucks (And That's Why It Works)*, **Armand and Nick provide data-backed frameworks to get past the initial knee jerk reaction and establish yourself as a peer**, even when you're calling a complete stranger.

–Matt Dixon,
Bestselling Author of *The Challenger Sale and The Jolt Effect*

Most sellers waste their cold calls with junk by asking prospects silly questions like how their day is going or trying to confirm their name or role—and they COMPLETELY waste their prospect's time. **Armand and Nick teach you to establish credibility in the first 60 seconds of a cold call** by demonstrating that you know their business and can offer value to them as a peer, simply by highlighting a problem so specifically that it becomes mind-numbingly obvious that you could help them in their business. That's how you cold call.

—Keenan,
Bestselling Author of *Gap Selling*

Armand and Nick are true practitioners who live and breathe what they train and share content around, especially when it comes to cold calling. **This is the most tactical, relevant, and actionable book I've ever read on the topic.** Their techniques and structure will teach anyone how to be a master cold caller if they're willing to put in the work. Cold calling isn't dead, it just needs to evolve, and this book is the evolution.

—John Barrows,
CEO of JB Sales,
(Sales Trainer to Salesforce, LinkedIn, Amazon, Google)

Most sales books are filled with fluff, stories no one cares about, and psychology without practical application. **Nick and Armand have, hands down, written THE best book out there on cold calling.** Now go hit the phones and use these tactics to land a s*** ton of meetings!

—Jason Bay,
CEO of Outbound Squad and Contributing Book Editor,
(Sales Trainer to Gong, Zoom, Rippling, Monday.com)

(But what about the sellers and leaders? Keep going!)

PRAISE FROM THE TOP 1% OF REVENUE LEADERS AND SELLERS

Best sales book of 2024: *Cold Calling Sucks (And That's Why It Works).* Few people on Earth have had more conversations with experts on cold calling than Armand and Nick. Even fewer people on Earth have scoured 300M+ cold calls to prove that their advice was right. Hopefully, more than a few people on earth will read this book and up their cold calling game and results.

–Mark Kosoglow,
CRO at Catalyst, Former VP of Sales at Outreach

To become the #1 rep, you need to build a plan and show up every day, especially when you don't feel like it. And for top sales performers, the plan should always include prospecting. This is one of the most actionable sales books you'll ever read, with talk tracks, voiceovers, and frameworks for cold calling that'll fuel your path to becoming a top sales performer. Best of all, this book provides proven systems to make sure you actually pick up the phone everyday, even when cold calling sucks (which it always does).

—Ian Koniak,
#1 Enterprise Rep at Salesforce

Most sales books are theoretical and based on opinions. For modern sellers to succeed in the AI era, they require data-backed guidance that empowers them to adapt their strategies and techniques to produce game-changing results. That's exactly what this book delivers. Through deep analysis of more than 300 million cold calls, it delivers a new gold standard for sales engagement that will supercharge pipelines for revenue teams at large enterprises and startups alike.

—Amit Bendov,
Founder and CEO of Gong

The cold calling advice in this book is based on proof, not preference. Way too many people give cold calling advice based on opinions that fell out of date 15 years ago. Not only are the tactics backed by data, but they also address the psychology of what it means to sell in a way that doesn't feel like selling. The game has changed and Armand and Nick have mastered it.

—Kevin "KD" Dorsey,
CRO (2x Unicorns, 4x 100+ People Orgs),
CEO of Sales Leadership Accelerator

When I first started as an SDR (and then as an SDR leader), I tried dozens of podcasts and sales books -- everything was out of date or irrelevant. I've never found something as impactful as the folks at 30MPC and their content. They have that rare ability to create break down practical, tactical content from real world sales practitioners. **This book on cold calling should really be retitled** *The Cold Calling Bible*.

—Ken Amar,
#1 All-Time SDR and Leader at Outreach,
Contributing Book Editor

COLD CALLING SUCKS

(And That's Why It Works)

Backed by **GONG**
Data on 300M+
Cold Calls

COLD CALLING SUCKS

CALLING

SUCKS

(And That's Why It Works)

A STEP-BY-STEP GUIDE TO
CALLING STRANGERS IN SALES

Armand Farrokh and Nick Cegelski

COLD CALLING SUCKS (AND THAT'S WHY IT WORKS)
A Step-by-Step Guide to Calling Strangers in Sales

For permission requests, speaking inquiries, podcast interviews, and bulk order purchase options, visit 30mpc.com/book.

30 Minutes to President's Club (30MPC)
3400 Cottage Way
Sacramento, CA 95825

This book wouldn't have been possible without our 3rd cofounder, Sean Yuan, who solves every other problem you could imagine at 30 Minutes To President's Club.

Designed by Transcendent Publishing | TranscendentPublishing.com
Edited by Lori Lynn Enterprises

30MPC.com

ISBN: 979-8-9911569-0-5

This publication is designed to provide helpful information on the subject matter covered (usually, cold calling). This book is not meant to be used, nor should it be used, to diagnose or treat any medical condition (because it's a book about cold calling). The advice and strategies contained herein may not be suitable for your situation (don't try the permission based opener on a rhinoceros). Neither the publisher nor the author shall be liable for any loss of profit or any other commercial damages, including but not limited to special, incidental, consequential, personal, or other damages (so if you cold call someone from the mafia ... that's your problem!) Readers should also be aware that the websites, links, and videos listed throughout this book may change or become obsolete (you know, especially if cold calling actually becomes dead in the year 2372).

Human Translation: We're gonna give you advice about cold calling. Come on, don't sue us for nonsense, folks!

"You don't have to feel good to get started, but you do have to get started to feel good."

CONTENTS

5 MINUTES TO FIGURE OUT
IF THIS BOOK IS WORTH YOUR TIME

Agenda

- Why should you cold call at all?
- Why should you believe anything we're saying?
- What can you expect from this book?

"**O**kay, bud. What's your secret?"

The new VP of Sales in town, Stef, was doing everything he could to figure out why only 1 in 4 reps were hitting their number. So he sat down every single rep that hit quota and drilled them with questions, one by one.

Six months prior, it was different. You had to be a complete buffoon not to hit quota.

The startup was red hot, and there were so many inbound leads that reps had no reason to hunt for their own business. The CEO would literally compare the reps to bears sitting by a river with salmon jumping into their mouths.

But he wanted hungry bears.

So he doubled the sales team in 6 months to spread those inbound leads razor thin. As expected, quota attainment plummeted to the floor.

One would think the old-guard reps might do some outbound prospecting to fill the gap. Nope. Instead, they preferred to rip on the new hires that ruined the good days. Maybe they hoped that the unwelcome environment and miserable paydays would make the new blood quit (they did) and convince management that they should stop hiring (they didn't).

"Who's that idiot making cold calls over there?"

That idiot was me—one of the lucky new hires.

Fortunately, I previously sold insurance in a 100% commission, 100% outbound role. The thought of someone reaching out to me to buy my product was completely foreign. So I'd eat the free inbound fish they gave me, then make 200 dials per week to find even more.

And after 6 months, one hungry idiot bear topped the leaderboard:

Armand Farrokh—Q1 2019 Attainment—264%

"Stef, it's really simple. I prospect more than anyone else on this floor."

I pulled up a Salesforce dashboard titled *AE Pipeline Generated* where one bar on the chart stuck out hilariously like a sore thumb.

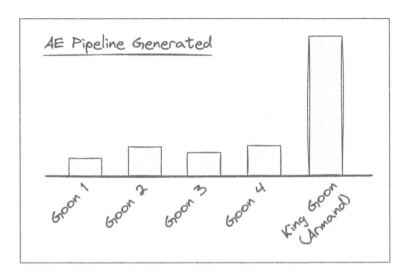

It was, quite literally, 4 times the pipeline of the next best rep (to this day, I still have no idea what the hell they were doing for 40 hours per week).

"But John says that he prospects just as much as you?" He referred to the only other seller with a reputation for outbound prospecting.

"He does. Almost. We both reach out to about 50 companies per week. But the difference is John mostly sends cold emails. I do that too, but I make *a lot* of cold calls."

I continued, "I book 8 outbound meetings per week. 4 come from the phone and 4 come from email. So even against the next best outbounder on this team, I'm wringing twice as much juice out of every account in my territory."

I walked Stef through every part of my prospecting process. His eyes lit up. It was the first *repeatable* sales process he'd seen in all his interviews.

Every other old-guard AE said that the only way to succeed was to sit on a goldmine territory and survive long enough to build up referral flow from your existing customers.

But when you get good at cold calling, you realize it's quite formulaic.

Opener. Pitch. Objections. Meeting.

It wasn't fun, but anyone could learn how to do it with the right pieces.

Three months later, Stef came back around and sat me down again.

"You're running the SDR org, bud."

Guess his turnaround plan was … me?

He put me in charge of 20 sales development representatives—the entry-level sellers who have one job and only one job: booking outbound meetings for the closers.

And over the next year, we doubled the SDR team but *tripled* their pipeline generation.

Why? Because we taught them to pick up the damn phone.

Cold Calling Sucks, and That's Why It Works

Success in sales is determined by the number of uncomfortable conversations you're willing to have.

There's no place this rings truer than in cold calling.

Cold calling is painful and uncomfortable for every single salesperson on planet Earth. Most will do anything to avoid it.

And while this book will teach you some ways to make it *less* painful, you're in for a rough ride if you're not prepared to accept the following reality:

Cold Calling Sucks (And That's Why It Works), and there's nothing you can do to change that. But that's exactly why it works.

No matter how good you get, you're gonna be sworn at, told to *get a real job*, and treated like dirt by folks who wouldn't dare say those things if you were meeting them face-to-face.

Your average seller makes a couple dials, hits 6 voicemails, and gets their heart ripped out when the next prospect tells them to screw off … so they give up!

Then, they disguise their fear and anxiety in behaviors like:

- Complaining that cold calling is dead and no one answers the phone anymore
- Spending hours over-researching prospects who haven't even answered yet
- Claiming it's end of quarter, so there's no time to prospect
- Following up with long-dead opportunities
- Checking their inbox 20 times a day
- Updating the CRM
- Scheduling cold calls at the "optimal time to "dial"
- "Social Selling"

Why? Because there's an easy route.

Nowadays, you can send 400 prospecting emails with a click of a button without taking any interpersonal risk.

The problem is that *because* blasting cold emails is so easy, thousands of other sales reps are flooding your prospect's inboxes every single day.

Prospects open their inbox and bulk delete 20 of them as if it were their morning routine.

They're getting bombarded with so many sales emails that it's becoming harder and harder to cut through the noise, regardless of how "personalized" your emails are.

And when your quota is based on the *average* performance of reps on your team, you literally cannot beat the average if all you do is blast cold emails like everyone else.

Few salespeople are willing to submit themselves to the discomfort of cold calling consistently, which makes your competition extremely slim.

There's no avoiding the suck of cold calling. But every time you decide to pick up the phone despite the suck, you separate yourself from the pack just a little bit more.

You can *still* play the game of who can send the best 400 emails per week, then every meeting you book from cold calling is gravy on top.

> **Cold emails can get you to quota. But cold calls will get you to President's Club.**

The Math of a Top Quartile Cold Caller

Every day, you'll see a new "hot take" from someone on LinkedIn claiming that "cold calling is dead."

And yes, if you try cold calling for two weeks and quit … your numbers will absolutely suck.

However, if you stick it out and commit to mastering your craft (which is what you're doing now by opening this book), you *will* reach the top 25% of cold callers.

But is that even worth it?

Let's find out. Assume you make 200 dials per week for an entire month.

Using data from over 300 million cold calls recorded on Gong's revenue intelligence platform to analyze buyer-seller interactions, let's compare the difference between the average rep and the top quartile rep.

	Average Rep	Top Quartile Rep
# Dials[1]	800	800
# Connects[a]	43 (5.4%)	106 (13.3%)
# Meetings Booked[a]	2 (4.6%)	18 (16.7%)

The data shows that, for every 800 dials, the number of connects for the average rep is 43 compared to the top quartile rep at 106. And the average rep books two meetings whereas the top 25% rep books a whopping 18 meetings from the same number of calls.

(And if you thought the top 25% reps booked a lot of meetings … the *top 10%* of reps book even more—1 meeting for *every 3 cold calls* that connect.)

So yeah, it sucks to be *average* at cold calling.

But if you learn to dial smart and master the craft … there are very few places where you can book an extra 18 meetings per month off just an hour of work per day.

And that's why you're here: to be a top quartile dialer (not an average one).

---

[1] Data provided by Gong, citing the 50th and 75th percentile of sales reps.

But wait, there's more! It's not just the meetings you'll get *on* the calls.

Cold calling nearly doubles your email reply rate even if you don't connect live.

	Without Cold Calls	With Cold Calls
Email Reply Rate	1.81%	3.44% (1.9x higher)

Every cold call you make and voicemail you leave draws attention back to your emails, so you book *even more* meetings across other channels.

Between those 18 extra meetings a month *and* whatever comes from the increase in your email reply rate of every email you send …

You're telling me it's not worth one hour a day to cold call?

Four Promises for the Most Actionable Book in Sales

 Most sales books are a slew of random tips masquerading as advice. You read hundreds of pages filled with "hot takes" that cover up the fact that the author can't actually break a sales call down step-by-step.

Maybe you finish the book feeling excited about the concept of cold calling, but then you realize when you pick up the phone, *you have no idea what you should actually say.*

The world does not need more advice. It needs more structured advice. This book is structured to be the most actionable sales book in the world.

Here are our four promises to make that happen:

#1) We broke down every part of a cold call, step-by-step.

We'll assemble the pieces of a cold call in chronological order like this:

- **Section 1 teaches you to nail the first 60 seconds.** Specifically, what the heck do you say when you open a cold call, and how do you pitch your product?
- **Section 2 covers the rest of the call.** Three steps to handle *any* objection, talk tracks for 18 of them, tactics to bypass gatekeepers, and ways to maximize voicemail replies.
- **Section 3 finishes with how to be a machine.** How to get more meetings in fewer dials and make more dials in less time without sacrificing quality.

No matter how good you get at cold calling, you will get stuck at *some* point. Whenever that happens, you'll never have to guess what chapter to revisit.

#2) You'll *hear* voiceovers (embedded in QR codes) that allow you to master the tone.

Much of the nuance of a cold call is not just what you say but *how you say it*—aka, your tone. You can say the exact same words as the #1 seller, but if you talk too fast, use too many uptones, or sound like a robot, your prospect will be able to tell.

We recorded voiceovers for every talk track so you know exactly how you should sound when the words come out of your mouth. You'll notice we don't always stick to the script word-for-word. It's okay to alter your talk tracks for what feels most natural in the moment.

To listen, just scan the QR codes or go to 30mpc.com/guide to access all the talk tracks, data charts, and drawings in one place.

#3) You'll be covered, no matter what you sell.

We've built the #1 podcast in sales, with millions of downloads per year. We've done over 200 interviews with elite sellers who made President's Club at all levels, from VPs of Sales to SDRs to insurance agents to managers and everything in between.

While those guests predominantly come from tech, this book will work *anywhere*.

As a VP of Sales, I led a fast-paced startup from $100k to $13M+ in ARR, but I cut my teeth selling insurance in my first sales job. Nick was a multiple-time #1 enterprise rep selling old-school accounting software to attorneys, but today, he sells advertising sponsorships for us.

Moreover, our audience consistently tells us that they steal the stuff from the best reps in tech (which tend to be ahead of the game) and use it in another industry to gain an unfair advantage.

But to go the extra mile for this book, we took our experiences and our guests' experiences *and* enlisted audience editors from different sales environments to ensure these concepts work *everywhere*:

- **In every industry**. The insights come from elite reps who've sold SaaS, sponsorships, insurance, real estate, pharma, elevators (yup), cell phone towers, and more.
- **At every company**. At companies like Salesforce, Keller Williams, LinkedIn, Gong, Northwestern Mutual … and dozens of SMBs with no brand recognition at all.
- **With every prospect**. With customers in HR, finance, legal, engineering, government, homeowners, and ordinary people in the US, Canada, Europe, Asia, and beyond.
- **At every level**. With advice that teaches even the #1 rep something new while still being accessible to a new grad with zero sales experience.

While the products, personas, and industries might change, the underlying principles will apply whether you're selling software, real estate, insurance, pipe cleaners, or dog food.

#4) You'll find data to back it all up.

There's so much unsubstantiated advice out there that *sounds* good but sucks in practice. We partnered with Gong to back the advice with data from over *300 million* cold calls.

Their dataset comes from running the #1 revenue intelligence platform to engage prospects, analyze sales calls, and forecast deals for over 4,000 sales teams across industries.

And no, they didn't pay to be in the book.

We picked them because they're the single most trusted source for sales data, as proven by the fact that they run the #1 data-backed blog in sales.

You'll find data that not only helps you benchmark your call success but also validates the specific talks we cite.

Do Not Use This Book as an Excuse

Before you embark on your cold calling journey, I want to underscore one thing. There is no book, podcast, course, or training in the world that'll teach you more than actually making cold calls.

We didn't write this as an exercise in sales academia. We wrote it to get you to President's Club. The only way you'll learn what actually works is by putting the lessons into action and making *real* cold calls at the end of every chapter instead of hiding behind a book.

So, we're providing two free resources below that will allow you to take action *today*.

1. **A basic cold calling framework** you can use to win the first 60 seconds of a call. I used this framework when I sold legal software and still use it to sell 30MPC sponsorships today.

2. **Our cold calling playbook episode from the podcast,** which breaks down the key parts of a cold call step-by-step—including how you should *sound* on the phones.

This won't cover every opener you could use or objection you'll need to handle, but it's absolutely enough to get started.

So scan the QR codes on the next page and queue them up for your next commute to work.

Let's get ready to hit the phones.

Your Minimum Viable Cold Calling Resources

Resource #1: Your Minimum Viable Cold Calling Framework	
You (Tailored Permission Opener): Emma, I just finished reading your press release about your new office opening.	**Lead with context**
I'm gonna be honest, this is a cold call, but it is a well-researched one.	**Own the cold call**
Can I get 30 seconds to tell you why that press release prompted me to call you specifically, then you can tell me whether or not it makes sense for us to speak?	**Get permission to pitch**
Prospect: Sure.	
You (Problem Proposition): The reason I'm calling you is, most of the CFOs of insurance defense law firms think it's ridiculous that they have to deal with so many deductions, rejections, and appeals they get from insurance carriers after winning a big case.	**Triggering problem**
We help other insurance defense law firms cut down on bill appeals by alerting attorneys to billing guideline violations right when they're doing their time entries …	**One-sentence solution**
And I'm wondering if you might be open to learning more when I'm not completely calling you out of the blue?	**Interest-based CTA**

Resource #2: The Cold Calling Playbook Episode

PRO TIP: Find an Accountability Partner

As we said, cold calling is really hard. You might be on a sales floor where you're the only one owning your professional development. If that's the case, then congrats to you. We hope this book becomes your unfair advantage that gets you to #1 on the leaderboard.

But there's usually *at least* one other person on the team who's getting after it like you.

You'll retain much more information (and have more fun along the way) if you read this with your cold calling partner in crime.

- You'll hold each other accountable to 200 dials this week.
- You'll role-play a new opener or objection.
- You'll laugh off the most ridiculous prospect reactions.
- You'll coach each other's calls and get out of the echo chamber of your brain.

Nick and I don't do the whole "read every chapter together" thing so that we can read at our own pace. But whenever we finish, we have a shared language of concepts that we can reference in the game of sales and business to win together every day.

If you've got two thumbs and a friend, shoot out a few text messages and see if they'll join you for the ride.

But don't let that stop you from reading Chapter 1 now.

THE FIRST 60 SECONDS

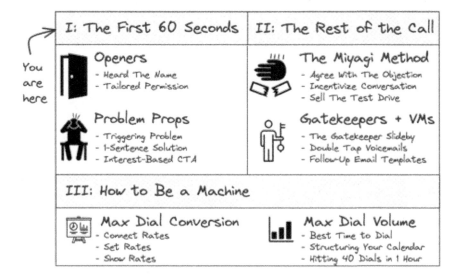

Most cold calls are won or lost within the first 60 seconds.

They end in brisk hang-ups and dismissals because every seller is using the same openers, making the same tone mistakes, and using the same buzzword-filled pitches that immediately categorize you as a telemarketer.

The goal of the first 60 seconds is to *earn* the next 60 seconds. If you can get past the first 60 seconds, that's when you're actually having a conversation instead of being brushed off.

And the way you do that is by mastering the two components that comprise the first minute of a cold call.

Chapter 1 covers openers. How do you get a complete stranger to hear you out when you called them out of the blue?

Chapter 2 covers problem propositions. How do you talk about your product in a way that doesn't make you sound like a Billy Mays commercial?

Let's dive in.

OPENERS

Agenda

- Why most cold calls are lost in the first 30 seconds
- The "Heard The Name Tossed Around?" Opener
- The Tailored Permission Opener

 "Hi, this is Armand from Northwestern Mutual. How's your day going?"

Click

God, this job f***ing sucks.

It was my first ever sales job and it felt like hang-up #772. I was a month into my college internship selling insurance, and I couldn't book a meeting to save my life.

At the start of the internship, you'd assemble a list of 200 people you knew who might be interested in financial planning. But when you're 19, that list runs dry pretty early on.

You call your parents … then your uncle … then your cousin … then your barber … and next thing you know, nobody wants to talk to you at Thanksgiving.

Most interns burn through their warm network in a month, then quit. But I was broke and I needed money, so after finding a new barber (literally), I decided to go cold. Every day, I would pick a new law firm in Los Angeles and cold call every single partner in the building.

Never in my life have I been verbally eviscerated so badly.

800 dials. 0 meetings booked. I lost every call in the first 60 seconds.

They'd answer in a semi-friendly tone, but the moment I asked, "How's your day going?" their tone of voice would shift. I could suddenly feel their impatience brewing like I was on a cold calling shot clock. It's like they could *smell* the young, inexperienced, desperate life insurance salesman through the phone.

From there, they'd rip me apart. One guy said, "There's no way in hell I'm taking your money advice." Another, immediately after my opener, said, "Go get a real job, kid," and hung up.

As hardheaded as I was, I was starting to believe they were right. I felt like I was slowly turning into the one thing nobody ever wants to be: a telemarketer.

And just as I was getting ready to call it quits, a top producer named Brandon Hoffman walked by and had a brief conversation with me that changed my life.

*   *   *

Brandon was one of the rare survivors in the feast-or-famine game of insurance. Most reps barely paid their rent, but the few that made it to the top? They were grossing 7 figures.

He was only 32, but I'm telling you, when the guy walked by, he *smelled* like money. Slicked back curly hair, Rolex watch, the letters "BH" stitched into the cuff of his custom navy suit, and one of the few guys who could get away without wearing a tie in the office.

When he walked by, the entire intern floor was empty except for a lone idiot (me) making cold calls to pay for a $5 footlong at Subway. To be honest, I think he felt bad for me. So he stopped by to give me some advice.

"Hey man, it's gonna be really hard to get anyone to take money advice from you."

(Yeah, great advice dude.)

"But you're working hard."

"Thanks, man, I'm trying."

"If I were in your shoes, I'd call all the partners in the Skadden Law office and say, 'I work with a few other partners in the office. It's Brandon Hoffman from Northwestern. Have you heard my name tossed around?'"

"But I don't work with any of those people. And they *definitely* have not heard my name tossed around."

"They probably haven't heard mine either. It doesn't matter. It's about showing that you work with other people of their stature. That's the difference between a telemarketer and an advisor."

He continued, "Bring me along. I'll close the deals, and we'll split them 50/50. If they want references, I'll share them live. But they're not even gonna remember what you said on the call."

He walked away with the final words, "Just give it a shot, kid. What do you have to lose?"

I was massively skeptical. The line felt like a cringey flex. But he was right. I had nothing to lose.

So I dropped my tone of voice three notches to sound like I was *at least* 23 and gave it a swing:

"Hey Bill, we work with a few other partners in the Skadden LA office. Armand from Northwestern, heard my name tossed around?"

"Well, no, I haven't. But how can I help you?"

Oh, friendly now, aren't we?

I didn't know what was supposed to come next. I'd barely made it this far in the past. So, I followed up with my mediocre but brief pitch: a one-sentence summary of how we help other law firm partners invest while saving on taxes.

I kid you not. Two minutes later, Bill booked the meeting.

I couldn't believe it. Same law firm. Same pitch. Same 19-year-old kid without confidence. Only one freaking thing changed: the way that I opened the cold call.

It had to be a fluke. I kept going.

"Heard the name tossed around?" Two meetings booked.

"Heard the name tossed around?" Three meetings booked.

40 dials in, I literally booked three meetings in a single session alone. More meetings in one hour than I had in the *entire* last four weeks of cold calling combined.

The entire demeanor of the cold call was changed by leading with social proof instead of introducing myself and asking, "How's your day going?" or "Did I catch you at a bad time?"

Even if I didn't book a meeting, the conversations would last longer because they didn't want to eviscerate someone who might work with one of their peers.

This got me to the *other parts* of the call so I could sharpen the pitch, practice the objections, and build a full playbook that allowed me to book meetings off 1 in 4 conversations.

But you need the opener to *gain access* to the next 60 seconds.

We'll break it down in just a few pages. But to do that, we need to explain why most cold call openers immediately categorize you as a telemarketer.

The Two Worst Ways to Open a Cold Call

 99.9% of cold calls come from unprofessional telemarketers, blindly dialing through the phone book trying to sell extended car warranties, sketchy business loans, and predatory student loan refinancing packages.

Like it or not, your prospect will lump you in with these folks when you call them, and it's your job to quickly disavow them of this perception.

When your prospect answers your cold call, their radar is on high alert for any cues that tell them you're another "worthless telemarketer" that they should hang up on.

- The overly chipper tone
- The slightest tremble in the voice
- The canned openers that everyone else uses
- The robotic pitch that shows you *obviously* didn't research them

Everything you do and say on a cold call must *sound* and *feel* different from the typical cold calls your prospect usually receives.

That's why the following two cold call openers are banned from your dictionary because they categorize you as a telemarketer within the first 5 seconds of a call.

Banned Opener #1: How's Your Day Going?

You and I both know you don't really care about the day of the person on the other end of the line. You're not calling random CFOs to inquire about the "quality" of their afternoon … you're trying to sell them something.

You know it, I know it, and *they* know it. Inevitably, what you'll hear in return is a deep sigh (because you're wasting their time), followed by, "I'm fine; what's this regarding?"

That's code for "What are you trying to sell me, telemarketer?"

Even if you are some sort of lunatic empath who actually cares about every prospect's day, it doesn't matter.

Nearly *every* salesperson uses this opener, and your prospect won't be able to distinguish your sincerity from every other call. It only lumps you in with the rest of the telemarketers.

Banned Opener #2: Did I Catch You at a Bad Time?

You're making a *cold* call. Of course, it's a bad time. I can't count the number of times I've heard a prospect say, "Yes, it's a bad time," then never answer your call again, as if they were part of the witness protection program.

This is the equivalent of the "Dear Sir/Madam" greeting. It lowers your status in the eyes of the prospect as if they'd be so gracious as to spare you a moment of their attention. It was clearly a good enough time for them to have answered the phone, so don't backtrack to ask them if you bothered them as if you were a pest.

And just like the last one, this is a dead giveaway that you're a telemarketer. You'll hear the exact same sigh because you've categorized yourself with the rest.

Bonus Banned Opener: Is This Bob?

This isn't really an opener, but it's worth calling out.

When you ask whether or not you have the right person, you make it *extremely obvious* that you don't actually know the person's voice and that you're a stranger (aka, a telemarketer). You're better off assuming you have the right person and going right into your *actual* opener.

Don't worry. If they're *not* the prospect you think they are, they'll correct you. It's better to deal with that occasional awkwardness than burn every prospect you call by asking them to confirm their name.

How Should You Open a Cold Call Instead?

 So, how do you avoid coming off like a telemarketer?

You open the cold call with context about *them*—a mutual investor, another partner you work with in the same office, a customer in the same industry, or anything that demonstrates that you're not a complete stranger.

Leading with context completely changes the demeanor of the call for three reasons.

1. **The Sit-Up Moment**. They sit up and realize you might actually work with their peers, so you're not a complete rando they can treat like trash without it coming back to them.

2. **Can't Be Canned**. Context-first openers *can't* be canned even if everyone in the world adopted them, because the context is unique to the prospect.

3. **Snap the Telemarketer Stigma**. You demonstrate that you took the time to research them in the first 5 seconds of a cold call, which sets you apart from the spam callers.

There are two context-first openers we'll provide to do this in practice. The "Heard The Name Tossed Around?" Opener and the Tailored Permission Opener.

And if you're skeptical, I get it. Maybe you haven't heard us talk about these openers before. You probably haven't seen them in the field. And when every other seller uses those traditional (banned) openers, you have every right to have your doubts.

Fortunately, you don't have to take our word for it. Here's the data from Gong about which cold call openers are most likely to convert to a meeting:

Opener[2]	Success Rate
BANNED: Did I catch you at a bad time?	2.15%
BANNED: How's it going?	7.60%
Permission-Based Opener	11.18%
Heard The Name Tossed Around	11.24%

But if you want to keep rolling with "Did I catch you at a bad time?" then be my guest.

For everyone else, let's go back to the Heard The Name Tossed Around Opener.

Opener 1: Heard The Name Tossed Around Opener

---

[2] Gong pulled key identifying phrases for each cold call opener, including similar variations (i.e., how's it going + how's your day going).

There are three main pieces to the opener, as broken down below:

Talk Track: The Heard The Name Tossed Around Opener	Steps
Hey Bill, we work with a few other partners in the Skadden LA office.	**Lead with context**
It's Armand from Northwestern …	**THEN intro yourself**
Heard the name tossed around?	**Heard the name?**

Lead with context before you say *anything else*, even your name. The first words that come out of your mouth determine whether or not the prospect listens to anything else you say.

To create the *sit-up moment*, you need to find a common thread between you and them. For me, it was the fact that we worked with other partners in their office.

But even when I was at a 9-employee company with under 50 customers, I could almost always find *some* common thread between my current customers (or even the open opportunities in my pipeline) and my prospects. Some examples include:

- **Same Investor**. "We work with a few other Sequoia portfolio companies."
- **Same Coworkers**. "We work with a few other partners in the Downtown LA office."
- **Same Situation** "We work with a few other multifamily homeowners down the block."

- **Same Industry Peers**. "We work with a few folks like Gong and Salesforce."
- **Same Geo + Persona**. "We work with other compensation leaders in Salt Lake City."

The more specific you can get, the better. You'll notice the last one was a combination of geography and persona to make it feel close to home. But opening with "we work with other professionals who breathe" isn't particularly compelling.

Now, **you're ready to introduce yourself and ask the question.** "It's Armand from Northwestern. Heard the name tossed around?"

The final question is the twist at the end of the punch. You already got Bill to sit up by telling him that you work with his peers, and now you're going to lean into it *even more*. We want him to think, *I haven't heard of them … but should I have?*

You can say all the right words, but if your tone sounds unsure or overly stiff like a telemarketer (aka, *not* a peer), this opener will fall flat.

Nailing the Tone: Heard The Name Tossed Around Opener

Imagine you're leaning back in the chair with your feet up on the desk. You should sound assumptive, as if you're *expecting them* to know you. Imagine you're calling a referral (*Hey Jane, we both know Nick. He gave you a heads up that I'd be calling, right?*)

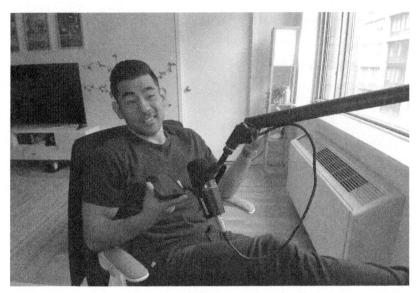

How I actually sat when recording this one—leaning back, feet up.

The two most common tone mistakes here are over-enunciation and upward inflection.

- **Over-enunciation** makes you sound stiff like you're reading off a billboard (*Welcome to this cold call, we work with a number of partners in the law firm!*)

- **Upward inflection** makes you sound unsure (*We work with a few other partners in the office? It's Armand ... at Northwestern Mutual?*)

Have a buddy record you having a normal conversation when you're not expecting it. Listen to that tape—that's *exactly* how you should sound on a cold call. Chances are, you sound much more casual, you end your sentences in a downtone.

This is much easier heard than written, so we've recorded two examples. A bad one using over-enunciation and upward inflection, and a better one using that "Feet-Up" tone.

Stiff (Bad) Example	Feet-Up (Good) Example

Scan the QR codes or access all talk tracks at 30mpc.com/guide.

Transitions After "Heard The Name Tossed Around?"

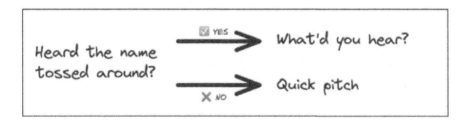

After you ask the question, they'll either answer yes or no. To be clear, it does not matter if they've heard your name tossed around. It's about making it seem like they *should have*.

The vast majority of people will say "no," so let's start there.

You *must* stay in character, even if they haven't heard your name tossed around. Joke and laugh as if they *should have* heard your name tossed around. If you come off as startled or suddenly stiff, you have revealed your "rando" mask.

I'll say something like:

- "Ha! Guess I'm not as popular as I thought. Well, the reason for my call is …"
- "Oh! Normally we would've crossed paths by now. Well, the reason for my call is …"

- "Huh! Well, we work with a few other partners in the office and the reason I called *you* is …"

From there, you go into a very short pitch (to be covered in the next chapter).

But if they *have* heard your name tossed around, then guess what? You don't need to pitch.

Instead, jump in with the following line: *"Oh good, we'd normally be working with someone like you by now. What'd you hear?"*

From there, they usually still have no clue what you do. So you end up giving the same pitch you'd give if they said no anyway.

✳   ✳   ✳

To recap, lead with context, introduce yourself, and then ask if they've heard your name tossed around.

From there, regardless of their answer, it's time to deliver your pitch, which we call a Problem Proposition. But hang tight because that's the topic of Chapter 2.

First, let's give you another opener that's quite different from my approach because it *leans into* the cold call …

The Tailored Permission Opener.

Opener 2: The Tailored Permission Opener

Mediocre telemarketers use false pleasantries to hide the fact that they're making a cold call, but a prospect can smell that nonsense from a mile away.

The Tailored Permission Opener works because it *owns* that you're making a cold call and disarms the prospect with brutal honesty.

There are three steps to this opener: lead with context (again), own the cold call, and then get permission to pitch. Here's what that looks like:

Talk Track: The Tailored Permission Opener	Steps
Emma, I just finished reading your press release about your new office opening.	**Lead with context**
I'm gonna be honest, this is a cold call, but it is a well-researched one.	**Own the cold call**
Can I get 30 seconds to tell you why that press release prompted me to call you specifically, then you can tell me whether or not it makes sense for us to speak?	**Get permission to pitch**

Just like the Heard The Name Tossed Around opener, lead with context in step 1 to differentiate yourself from the blind spam dialers.

The key here is to lead with context related to a problem you solve instead of a random piece of information (like their alma mater).

For example, when I sold accounting software to law firms, I would lead with things like:

- "I just read about the big case win" (which means they'd be collecting money).
- "I just saw you opened a new office" (which has tax implications).
- "I was reading up on the new litigation practice" (which adds billing complexity).

When you lead with context related to the problem you solve, it allows you to *attach* the context to your pitch, which we'll cover in the next chapter. That's far more powerful than saying, "Hey, I noticed you went to LSU," then randomly transitioning to a pitch on billing software.

After leading with context, we'll come clean that this is indeed a good ol' cold call.

"I'm gonna be honest, this is a cold call, but it is a well-researched cold call."

There's a reason prospects often angrily react to calls with, "Is this a cold call!?"

They *know* it's a cold call! And it pisses them off when you try to mask your intentions with pleasantries and schmoozing. That's why they'll call you out even *more* aggressively out of spite.

But it's hard to get mad when you *acknowledge* that you're interrupting their day.

You reveal the human behind the phone because your words and tone read: *No one loves cold calls. I get it. But hear me out because I'm the only one who actually took a second to learn something about you before I called.*

You'll run the risk of coming across as low-status if you sound timid or ashamed when you fess up that it's a cold call. You can prevent that from happening by confidently leaning into humor here. Try phrases like:

- "I know I'm an interruption."
- "I hate to break it to you, but this is a cold call."
- "You're probably gonna hate me for this, but this is a cold call."

Sound a little cheeky and like you're having a fun time here, not like you're terrified of the prospect, and you'll *increase* your status.

Last, ask for permission to pitch and give them perceived control.

"Can I get 30 seconds to tell you why that press release prompted me to call you specifically, then you can tell me whether or not it makes sense for us to speak?"

Make it clear exactly how long you need and that you'll let them decide if they want to keep talking after those 30 seconds. It feels counterintuitive, but when your prospect has a say over the outcome of the call, they feel safe to agree to hear and *actually listen to* your pitch.

They'll almost always let you proceed, and some will even reply tongue-in-cheek with, "Alright, I'm counting *exactly* 30 seconds."

You've turned their brain back on. They're not confused about what you want or fighting you to get off the phone. They're listening to your next 30 seconds to decide if what you sell is worth their time.

And it's all because you led with context, owned the cold call, and let them decide if they wanted to opt in to your pitch.

Nailing the Tone: The Tailored Permission Opener

If you come in overly chipper, gung ho, or intense, their guard will stay up because you *sound* like the telemarketer who'll pressure sell them no matter how they respond.

And if you sound scared or anxious, you'll seem too junior and low-status to hear out. **Instead, your tone should sound confident and like you're arms-up with nothing to hide**.

Me on a real cold call, arms-up, saying, "This is a cold call."

I literally put my arms up in the air when I say this opener.

It should sound like, *Hey, I know you don't love this; it is what it is, but at least I took the time to research you, unlike all the other goons.*

You want them to hear the human on the other line, but also feel like you understand that no one loves cold calls, and it's okay to say "no."

Here are some examples:

Chipper (Bad) Example	Arms-up (Good) Example

What Do You Do If They Say "No"?

NO! → 1: Not a priority? 2: Or too busy? → Want the pitch now or later?

When a prospect denies you permission to pitch, they're not objecting to your product. They're objecting to your *interruption* and swatting you away as a telemarketer.

You need to get a conversation going to break the telemarketer perception, so *incentivize* them to share more about why they wouldn't let you proceed by saying:

If They Deny Permission to Pitch (Part 1)	Steps
Shoot, my bad. Just so nobody from my team bugs you again …	*Provide an incentive*
Is it just that I caught you at a horrible time, or is it that you already know what we do, and this just isn't a priority at all?	*Give them two potential reasons*

It's critical you provide the incentive (no more cold calls!) for them to share more, otherwise they have no reason to stay on the line.

Almost no prospect will *really* know what you do, so from there, it almost doesn't matter what they say. You'll respond with something like:

If They Deny Permission to Pitch (Part 2)	Steps
I appreciate you being upfront. To be honest, I don't really love making these calls and I'm sure you're not a fan, either. Look, I did my research on ya and this isn't just a random call. Could I take 30 seconds to share what I found and then you can totally hang up on me if it's not relevant?	*Reveal the human behind the phone*

Use humanizing language and reiterate that this isn't a random spam dial to increase your chances of getting another 30 seconds.

What About the (Untailored) Permission-Based Opener?

There will be times that you either can't find observable information about your prospect to include in your opener, or you just don't have time to do the research.

In that event, you'll still find success with an untailored, traditional permission-based opener, which sounds something like:

Talk Track: The Untailored Permission Opener	Steps
Emma, my name's Nick with 30MPC. You're gonna hate me, but this is indeed a cold call.	*Own the cold call (no context)*
Mind if I take 30 seconds to share why I called you specifically, and then you can totally hang up on me if it doesn't make sense to speak from there?	*Get permission to pitch*

This one is less effective than the Tailored Permission Opener since there's no context. Your prospect has no idea why you're calling—you could be selling accounting software, or you could be calling from a collections agency. You run the risk that they *don't* give you permission or get caught completely off guard and interrupt you halfway through your pitch.

But if you didn't have the time to research or couldn't find anything, this one isn't bad.

*   *   *

These openers get you past the first 30 seconds of a cold call, but now it's on you to explain to your prospect what the heck you do. This is where most sales reps inadvertently re-categorize themselves as telemarketers by hurling their "pitch" or "value proposition" at their prospect.

In the next chapter, we'll throw your traditional value proposition in the trash. Chapter 2 is all about the Problem Proposition.

Top 4 Actionable Takeaways from Chapter 1

- **Avoid these two openers**: "How's your day going?" and "Did I catch you at a bad time?" because they immediately categorize you as a telemarketer. Never use them.

- **Lead with context.** You can break the telemarketer perception in the first five seconds by leading with something you know about them.

- **The Heard The Name Tossed Around Opener**. Lead with context, then introduce yourself, then ask if they've heard your name tossed around.

- **The Tailored Permission Opener**. Lead with context, own the cold call, then get permission to pitch.

CHAPTER 1 HOMEWORK:
THE STREETS OF SAN FRANCISCO

You see a tourist trolley. I see cold call practice.

In my voiceover of the Heard The Name Tossed Around Opener, you might've noticed some intentional stutters and "um's" to make it sound natural—as if I'm actually calling a referral out of the blue.

That's 100% by design. The stutters always fall in the exact same place every single time I say it because I've said the opener over 10,000 times (literally).

You might be thinking: "There's no way you practiced your opener on 10,000 prospects." If so, you're absolutely correct.

You don't need to connect with 10,000 prospects to practice your opener 10,000 times. If you only practiced on prospects, you'd have to make 2,000 cold calls to get 100 reps in. You can accomplish that in a single hour of solo practice.

When I was in my first AE role in San Francisco, I'd walk to work with a Jabra headset on, but there wouldn't be anyone on the other line.

I'd repeat the Heard The Name Tossed Around Opener over and over again until I could get it to sound perfectly smooth.

Your homework is to practice your opener 100 times on your next commute. I'm dead serious. Turn off the music in your car or walk the streets with a headset on. 100 reps.

Your opener will sound canned if you only practice on prospects.

THE PROBLEM PROPOSITION

Agenda
• Why traditional value propositions and pitches suck
• The Problem Proposition
• How to ask for the meeting

 **B**ack in college, Nick and I started a business called SuppNow, a nutrition supplement vending machine that could sell massive tubs of protein inside your gym to put GNC and Vitamin Shoppe out of business.

But vending a two-pound canister of Optimum Nutrition Whey is far more challenging than you might think. A regular soda machine can't withstand the force of a massive tub barreling through its gears. So we toured dozens of vending machine manufacturers until we found one who could build a custom vending machine for us.

From there, we cold called every gym in the Los Angeles area and landed our first location at a powerlifter's gym in Hollywood (for the record, we did it all using the Heard The Name Tossed Around opener … and no ever heard "SuppNow" tossed around).

Delivery day came along. The forklift driver gently guided the machine into the lobby and turned it on. Our eyes lit up. *We're gonna be millionaires.*

If only that goddamn machine could actually dispense a tub of protein.

Exhibit A: a piece of crap.

Over the next six months, we would get a weekly call from the gym owner, Olga, a stout Russian lady who sounded like she was ready to beat me up with a broomstick.

"YOUR MACHINE IS S***." A gentle reminder from Olga.

"Hey Nick, it's your turn." Today, he was on SuppNow repair duty.

He'd receive my jarring text in the middle of his WRITING-201 lecture and whisper, "Hey, can I get your notes later?" to a deeply confused classmate.

From there, he'd leave the classroom, bike all the way back to our off-campus apartment, load up the car with a few extra tubs of protein, and begin a 60-minute commute in prime time LA traffic from USC to Hollywood.

After enduring a 10-minute verbal barrage from Olga, he'd begin diagnosing all the ridiculous reasons that a $15,000 hunk of steel could not vend a tub of protein.

One day, the vending mechanism jammed *on* a tub of protein, causing it to erupt and cake the entire machine in white vanilla whey protein powder.

The next week, a lady purchased a multivitamin but instead got a bottle of Opti-Men (a multivitamin for men) and was extremely offended.

I thought that one was funny.

The issue was we *wanted* to expand but couldn't because of these horrible machines.

I looked at dozens of other machines and found out that most custom vending machines were made from the same base parts, which meant they'd all have the same issues with vending big products, including massive tubs of protein.

Until one day, a guy from a competing vending machine manufacturer called me.

I gave him a friendly opening reply. "Oh good, wanna sell me another broken machine?"

"Haha. Well, I'm reaching out because I noticed your machine was made by Vendico, and a lot of their customers get tired of jammed products, misvends, and angry support calls. Our machines actually work and I wanted to show you one of ours."

I didn't believe him. "Sorry, man, that's what they said too."

He didn't pitch. Instead, he listed every problem he'd seen with Vendico machines.

"Those protein tubs probably get stuck between the elevator and the wall." Check.

"Misvends because you have to use two slots for one big product?" Check.

"Can't stock more than three units without overloading a shelf?" Check.

What the hell? Did he have access to our support logs?

He had my attention because he was the first vending machine manufacturer who could call out the exact problems we were facing, but I still had no reason to believe why he'd be different.

In one sentence, he explained what *allowed* him to solve the problems. "You know those machines are all built from the same parts. But we designed every major vending system in our machines from scratch—slots to hold bigger products, stronger gears to push them, deeper elevator to prevent jams ... so that you can actually vend your protein."

He continued, "I don't expect you to believe me on a call. Could I show one of our machines in person so you can at least see it for yourself?"

I had no idea who this guy was. I'd never heard of his company. I knew *nothing* about his product other than the fact that it was a vending machine.

But I took the meeting.

Why? Because he described the problem so specifically that I *knew* he had seen something that other manufacturers hadn't seen (or weren't willing to tell me).

This is why you should dump your "value proposition" for a Problem Proposition.

If you can show a prospect that you understand the *problem* in excruciating detail, you barely need to talk about your *product* at all. Spend 80% of your time talking about the problem, then explain the unique differentiator that allows you to solve that problem in a single sentence.

Why "Value Propositions" and "Pitches" Suck

 The world has been conditioned to believe that the key to being a great seller is to have a phenomenal pitch. Next thing you know, your marketing team is teaching you how to deliver a "value proposition" filled with buzzwords and jargon that describe all of the amazing features your product has to offer.

Those value propositions usually sound like this:

- Acme is an all-in-one platform that streamlines your compensation planning process.
- Acme is the #1 real estate brokerage by transaction volume in Beverly Hills.
- Acme is your single source of truth for all of your financial transactions.

Unfortunately, your product has no "value" unless it's solving a problem.

There are three reasons why the traditional value proposition sucks.

1. **They often include vague telemarketer buzzwords**. Phrases like *single source of truth*, *all-in-one platform*, and *leading provider of X* trigger every telemarketer alarm because they're the same generic value phrases that reps use at every company.

2. **People act on problems more than benefits**. Human beings are more motivated to take action to get rid of pain than they are to achieve benefits. If someone has a headache, they're gonna take the Advil. But even if people know that there are health benefits to taking a multivitamin, people are far less likely to jump out of their seat to take one.

3. **Value has no context without a problem**. Unlike headaches, many outbound prospects need to be reminded of their problems before they can see the value of your solution. They won't care about your titanium-plated nonstick pan if they like their cookware. They will if you remind them that the egg stuck to their pan last week.

The pan doesn't matter until you remember this.

Still skeptical? Here's a list of products described in value vs. problem format.

Which column catches your eye?

Value Proposition	Problem
Easy dog food delivery service	Never carry kibble to your car again.
Speedy home cleaning	Let us deal with the scum behind the toilet.
Home laundry service	Are you gonna lose another sock this week?
Ergonomic insoles	If you're tired of taping heel blisters ...
Nose tape for clearer breathing	Who likes breathing through one nostril?
Eucalyptus cooling blankets	Waking up at 3 a.m. sweaty?

The problem wins every time.

It's on you to connect the dots for them by explaining a problem in such triggering detail that it becomes impossible to ignore your solution.

A triggering problem should transport them back to the crappiest part of their day when they thought *damn ... I really wish there was a way for me to not do this anymore.*

When you demonstrate that you understand the exact problem they're facing, you establish yourself as an industry insider who "gets" their business ... *not* a telemarketer.

If you nail the problem, you only need one sentence to describe your solution because all you need to say is that you can make the problem go away.

But I'm sure there are lots of folks who are *still* married to their single source of truth.

If you needed further evidence, we asked Gong to pull data on the part of the cold call where a rep was describing their product. **And you'll find that problem language is literally 3x more effective than the buzzword language often used in value propositions.**

Product Description	Success Rate
Buzzwords[3]	5.5%
Social Proof [4]	12%
Problem Language [5]	16%

On that note, let's walk through how to weave a triggering problem into your cold calls so you never have to use a value proposition again. It's called the Problem Proposition.

---

[3] Example buzzwords included: single source of truth, all-in-one platform, revolutionize.

[4] Example social proof language: mention of peer companies or customers (we helped [company] do ...).

[5] Example problem language: frustrated, anxious, hate, overwhelmed.

Introduction to the Problem Proposition

A Problem Proposition is a problem described in such triggering detail that all your prospect needs to hear is one sentence that makes it go away.

There are three parts to a good Problem Proposition, where the single most important point piece is nailing #1, the problem description.

Step 1: Triggering Problem. Describe the problem so specifically that it triggers the prospect, creating a visual of the crappy situation they've dealt with in the past. Using the vending machine example, you might say:

Typically when I'm talking to Vendico customers, they're sick of jammed products, glitchy touchscreens, and support calls because their machines aren't made to vend bigger products.

Step 2: One-Sentence Solution. In the format of "we do X so that the problem goes away," explain your biggest differentiator that *allows you to solve* that problem. Continuing the vending machine example:

We redesigned every problematic vending system in our machines so that you don't get a jam when you try to vend something bigger than a can of Pepsi.

Step 3: Interest-Based Call-to-Action (CTA): Instead of asking for a meeting (which feels heavy), see if they're interested in taking a look first. The final CTA sounds like:

My guess is you're all set. But open to taking a look so you know what's out there?

That's the problem prop. Describe the problem in triggering detail, give a one sentence solution for how you solve it, then ask if they're interested in learning more.

Let's break down each step so you can build a problem proposition for yourself.

Step 1: Triggering Problem

Most sellers *think* they're being specific enough about the problem but they're usually still using vague, fuzzy words that sound like mush to your prospect.

Your prospects have been long desensitized to the "saving money" claims since they heard their 3,000th Geico commercial telling them that 15 minutes could save them 15% or more on their car insurance.

Saving time or making money is not specific enough. You get drowned out in the ocean of telemarketers and commercials because every single solution in the world does 1 of 3 things: saves you time, makes you money, or mitigates risk. You need to be more specific.

For a problem to trigger a painful memory, you need to repaint the story as if you were describing a movie scene. That may include many of the following descriptors:

- **Persona**. Who felt the problem? (CFOs of NYC Law Firms, compensation leaders of Sequoia portfolio companies)
- **Annoyances**. What were they annoyed about? (bill rejections, support tickets)
- **Scenery**. What was the setting when it happened? (after a case win, tax day)
- **Emotion**. How would they describe the feeling? (frustrated, mind-numbing)

To illustrate this in practice, let's take a mediocre "base" problem statement and add each of the descriptors to that statement from when I was selling billing software to law firms:

Descriptor	Problem Statement
Base	Most CFOs tell us that billing takes a lot of time.
+ Persona	Most CFOs of Insurance Defense Law Firms tell us that billing takes a lot of time.
+ Annoyances	Most CFOs of Insurance Defense Law Firms tell us that billing takes a lot of time because of the deductions, rejections, and appeals.
+ Scenery	Most CFOs of Insurance Defense Law Firms tell us that billing takes a lot of time because of the deductions, rejections, and appeals they get from insurance carriers after winning a big case.
+ Emotion	Most CFOs of Insurance Defense Law Firms think it's ridiculous that they have to deal with so many deductions, rejections, and appeals they get from insurance carriers after winning a big case.

If you can't *see* the movie scene, it's not specific enough. Fortunately, you don't have to create a triggering problem out of thin air because your customers are *constantly* venting their issues on sales calls every day, and you can steal their words to build your problem proposition.

Be careful when using the same problems for different personas. For example, when I sold billing software to law firms, the problems varied depending on who I was talking to.

- **At the power line**. Billing Managers might complain about the day-to-day pain of having to manually edit and submit bills to client spend management portals.

- **Above the power line**. CFOs wouldn't care about the manual billing tasks since they're not in the weeds like the manager is. But they *would* complain about lost money from payment deductions and write-offs if bills weren't submitted in the proper format.

- **Another department**. Partners wouldn't even know about these billing headaches, but they'd absolutely care if the firm couldn't make capital investments due to outstanding or unpaid receivables.

Listen to the call recordings or talk with your customer success team to find out what *that specific persona* is complaining about.

That's your triggering problem.

And the best part is it's in the *prospect's language*, not sales language.

Step 2: One-Sentence Solution

 Because we've explained the problem in visceral detail, we only need to do two things to explain our solution in one sentence:

1. Tell them that we can solve the problem.
2. Give them the minimum level of detail that makes it believable (i.e., what is it about our solution that allows us to solve that problem).

It's critical to strike the balance between sharing too little and sharing too much.

If I said, "We help you save money on taxes," I would be sharing too little detail for my solution to be believable. For all they know, I could be a money-laundering financial guru who claims to have the secret methods of the rich, available to you for only six low payments of $69.95.

If I said, "We help you save money on taxes by putting your money in life insurance and allowing you to take out the gains tax-free," I would be sharing too much detail and *creating* objections because they might have an aversion toward life insurance as an investment vehicle.

The magic formula is "we do X so that the problem goes away," where X is your single biggest differentiator that allows you to solve the problem.

You'll be tempted to include every way that you solve the problem. *Don't.* Less is more. Instead, rely on the problem description and the way you've helped *other* people solve that problem (aka social proof) to fill in the gaps.

Here are some examples across various industries that strike the right balance:

- **Insurance**. We've helped other partners with a lot of things—investing, tax planning, etc.—so you don't have to give up half your paycheck every tax season.

- **Compensation Software**. We integrate with all your HR, equity, and performance platforms so you never have to plan compensation in spreadsheets again.

- **Real Estate**. We know most of the buyers in Redwood City and get all of them competing against each other so that you get top dollar when we list your property.

- **Legal Time Tracking Software**. We help firms like DLA Piper and Skadden cut down on bill appeals by flagging billing violations right as your attorneys enter their time.

- **High-Speed Wi-Fi**. We have the biggest fiber-optic network in Boston, so your game never drops again when your roommate turns on Netflix.

If we haven't beaten this to death enough yet, notice that we're *not* including any of the traditional billboard phrases that make you sound like Billy Mays selling Mighty Putty.

- **Buzz Words**. Avoid terms like single source of truth, all-in-one platform, single pane of glass. They're vague terms that mean nothing and scream telemarketer.

- **Categorizations**. Never put yourself in a product category like tax software, real estate agent, or CRM. If a prospect has one, they will dismiss you. Instead, focus on solving the problem they have, even if they have a solution in place.

- **Random Accolades**. No one cares if you've been in business since 1965 or if you're the leading provider of toilet paper unless it enables you to solve the problem better.

Mighty Putty's most commonly used benefit: pulling a truck.

Triggering problem? Check. One-sentence solution? Check. What's left? A call-to-action.

Step 3: Interest-Based Call-to-Action

Most salespeople are trained to use a call-to-action that sounds like:

- Are you free on Wednesday at 10 or 2 for a product demo?
- Would you like to meet with a specialist?
- When are you available for a 30-minute call?

These call-to-action statements all feel heavy. Why? Because they force your prospect to make multiple decisions at the same time.

- Do I care about this problem?
- Do I believe they can solve it?
- Do I want to meet with this salesperson?
- Am I free during those times?

A rule of thumb that spans all aspects of selling:

Only ask your prospect to make one decision at a time.

When you hit them with all four of these questions (subconsciously), they'll often say no to everything. Even if they *were* interested, they might say no because the thought of another meeting crowding their calendar is overwhelming, let alone one with a complete stranger.

The single most important thing is to validate their interest before anything else. Starting with a small ask (*Are you open to learning more?*) increases your chances of an initial yes, at which point you can inch forward and go for the meeting.

Here are a few ways you can phrase the interest-based CTA:

- My guess is this came out of left field for you, but open to learning more when I'm not calling you totally outta the blue?
- I'm sure you have something in place, but does any of that sound even moderately interesting to you?
- My guess is you're all set, but would you be opposed to taking a peek at what that looks like?

Within these examples, you'll notice three tricks that will make your ask sound less heavy.

1. **Use softening language** like "Would you be open to," or "Does that sound even *moderately* interesting?" instead of heavy language like "Are you interested?" or "Let's schedule a call."
2. **Use no-based questions** like "Opposed to learning more?" because prospects tend to feel safer when saying no (a la Chris Voss in *Never Split the Difference*[6]).

---

[6] Chris Voss, *Never Split the Difference: Negotiating as if Your Life Depended on It* (HarperCollins, New York, NY 2016).

3. **Use mini push-away statements** like "My guess is you're all set" or "I know this came out of left field" to reduce the pressure of the sale.

From here, if they say yes and validate their interest, it's time to book the meeting.

If they say no (which is usually what happens), that means they probably gave you an objection instead. Don't worry, though, we've got you covered. Chapter 3 is entirely devoted to handling objections like Mr. Miyagi.

How to Land the Meeting

Once you validate their interest, book the meeting to avoid an extended interruption.

While you *do* want to turn a cold call into a conversation, you don't want to turn a cold call into a 30-minute sales meeting. A scheduled meeting allows you to break the telemarketer stigma because you're no longer an interruption, and they'll actually be listening.

When you're asking for the meeting, suggest time ranges, not specific times. They're less likely to be free at a specific time. If you miss on the first try, they'll usually get impatient and say, "Just send me an email." And you'll never hear from them again.

Instead, call out the interruption and use that as an excuse to book a separate time.

Great, well, I know my call totally interrupted you, and I need to jump in a second myself. We can chat later this week—how's your Tuesday morning from 9–11 a.m. PST or Thursday afternoon from 2–4 PST?

Try to schedule it within the next 1–2 weeks. Per Gong data, the longer you wait, the less likely they are to show up.

Weeks from Cold Call to Meeting	Show Rate
Same week	54%
1 week out	53%
2 weeks out	53%
3 weeks out	49%
4 or more weeks out	32%

From there, confirm their email live. I've lost many meetings by assuming I had the right email address for my prospect, only to have my meeting invitation bounce as undeliverable.

The last piece is to explicitly ask them to accept your calendar invite once it hits their inbox. Gmail won't put the meeting on their calendar if you haven't previously exchanged emails, so they *have* to click accept for it to show up in their calendar.

Ideally, you send the meeting invite on the spot so that they can click accept live, but this won't always be realistic when you have a prospect rushing out the door, and you're scrambling to slap a title on the invite.

If they ask to coordinate times over email, always throw a dart at the calendar. It's psychologically easier to accept an existing calendar invite instead of adding a new one. But the moment you start going back and forth over email, the more likely they are to ghost you entirely.

Here's how you always leave with a meeting on the calendar:

Totally get it. Here's what I'll do—I'll throw a dart at the calendar for around this time later this week, along with some other times over email. Mind accepting the invite if it works or picking one of the backups if it doesn't?

Notice we're not asking for permission to send the invite. They have two options. Either accept the first time or pick a backup. Don't allow them to revisit the decision to schedule a meeting.

Putting It All Together (With Tone)

Before we move on to end-to-end examples, there are a few keys to nailing the tone when delivering a problem proposition.

You really want to join the ridiculousness of the triggering problem. If you're saying that "most partners find it absolutely ridiculous," you should sound like you believe it's absolutely ridiculous too. If you monotone your way through the problem, it won't sound like you actually empathize with their situation.

From there, you almost want to brush over your one-sentence solution. It should sound like, "So look, we do this thing to solve that problem," then transition *right away* into your push-away statement of "But my guess is you're probably set." This continues to remove the pressure of the sale and take the focus away from the product and onto the problem.

Lastly, shrug your shoulders during the interest-based CTA. It's almost like you're walking by a store with a friend, and you say, "Hey, wanna check it out just for kicks?" Don't make it sound like they're signing up for a big phone meeting.

In the next section, we'll run a few examples of the entire first 60 seconds together with your opener and a problem proposition. Listen very closely to the tone.

Example 1: Selling Billing Software to Law Firms

 Insurance companies require law firms to follow very strict rules when sending their bills. If an attorney sends a bill that uses even a single word that the insurance carrier doesn't pre-approve, the carrier can refuse to pay the bill!

Thus, CFOs of big law firms spend an inordinate amount of time reviewing and revising bills so that they don't get their bill rejected.

The Tailored Permission Opener here references a case win from their website, which usually means the firm gets to send their client a bill. From there, I highlight the most frustrating part of the billing process and include some brief social proof in my description of the solution.

You (Tailored Permission Opener): Emma, I just finished reading your press release about your new office opening.	**Lead with context**
I'm gonna be honest, this is a cold call, but it is a well-researched one.	**Own the cold call**
Can I get 30 seconds to tell you why that press release prompted me to call you specifically, then you can tell me whether or not it makes sense for us to speak?	**Ask for permission**
Prospect: Sure.	
You (Problem Proposition): The reason I'm calling you is most of the CFOs of insurance defense law firms think it's ridiculous that they have to deal with so many deductions, rejections, and appeals they get from insurance carriers after winning a big case.	**Triggering problem**
We help other insurance defense law firms cut down on bill appeals by alerting attorneys to billing guideline violations right when they're doing their time entries ...	**One-sentence solution**
And I'm wondering if you might be open to learning more when I'm not completely calling you out of the blue?	**Interest-based CTA**

Example 2: Selling Insurance to Law Firm Partners

 Going back to the insurance example, we'll lead with the Heard The Name Tossed Around Opener and include the fact that we work with other partners in their office, which creates a sit-up moment.

From there, we'll explain the triggering problem that other partners have, which is making way too much freaking money and giving half of it away every year.

Armand (Heard The Name Tossed Around Opener): Hey Nick, we work with a few other partners in the DLA Piper office.	**Lead with context**
It's Armand Farrokh from Northwestern.	**THEN intro yourself**
Heard the name tossed around?	**Heard the name?**
Nick (Prospect): I don't think I have. But how can I help you?	
Armand (Problem Prop): Oh! Guess I'm not as popular as I thought.	
Well, I work with a few other partners in the office, and you all have the wonderful problem of making so much money that you have to give 45% of it back in taxes every April.	**Triggering problem**
So we've helped them with a lot of things: investing, tax planning, etc.—so you don't have to give up half your paycheck anymore.	**One-sentence solution**
My guess is you've got this handled. But open to hearing more, if nothing else, so you know what's out there?	**Interest-based CTA**

Example 3: Selling 30MPC Sponsorships to Sales Tech Companies

 When I'm not writing, I sell our sponsorships for *30 Minutes to President's Club*. Most of our customers are Sales Tech companies that want to advertise on our podcast and newsletter.

This Tailored Permission Opener leads with a product release on their website, then transitions to the problem that we solve, which is making sure their product launch isn't a dud because they couldn't break through the noise. The one-sentence solution? A big announcement to over two million salespeople.

Nick (Tailored Permission Opener): Armand, I just finished reading about the launch of your new power dialing tool.	**Lead with context**
I'm gonna be honest: this is a cold call, but it is a well-researched cold call.	**Own the cold call**
Can I get 30 seconds to tell you why I called, then you can totally hang up on me if it doesn't make sense to speak from there?	**Ask for permission**
Armand (Prospect): Hah, fine. Go for it.	
Nick (Problem Prop): Usually, when I talk with CMOs of Sales Tech companies, they tell me it can be really frustrating to put a ton of work into a new product launch only to have it fall on deaf ears, since the sales tech space can get really noisy.	**Triggering problem**
About two million salespeople follow our podcast and newsletter series, and folks like Gong and Acme advertise with us to make sure their launches never fall flat.	**One-sentence solution**
I think our audience would be interested in your power dialer, and I'm wondering if you'd be against learning more sometime?	**Interest-based CTA**

Example 4: Selling Compensation Software to HR Leaders

 When I sold compensation software at Pave, we primarily targeted HR leaders at tech companies. Even if they weren't interested, they'd hear you out if you worked with a company that shared the same investors. That's what we'll reference in the Heard The Name Tossed Around Opener.

From there, the triggering problem is that HR leaders piece together separate confidential spreadsheets for every manager in the company to ensure compensation details don't get leaked. That means *hundreds* of spreadsheets for a 1,000-person company, which leads to serious compensation mistakes (and ulcers).

Armand (Heard The Name Tossed Around Opener): Hey Nick, we work with a few Sequoia portfolio companies.	**Lead with context**
It's Armand from Pave.	**THEN intro yourself**
Heard our name tossed around?	**Heard the name?**
Nick (Prospect): No, I haven't.	
Armand (Problem Prop): Oh! Well, I work with a few other Sequoia portfolio companies, and usually their Head of People Ops is buried under a mountain of spreadsheets during merit season in Q1.	**Triggering problem**
So they use Pave to pull their payroll, equity, and comp data into one place so you never have to run merit cycles in spreadsheets again.	**One-sentence solution**
I know you're probably a spreadsheet wizard. But open to taking a look so you know what's out there?	**Interest-based CTA**

And now, the game begins.

If you practice and nail the first 60 seconds, you shouldn't have to deal with nearly as many abrasive swats and hang-ups. But no matter what, you will still face objections even if you have the best opener and problem proposition in the world.

Don't worry, that's a *good thing*. An objection is the beginning of an actual conversation around the pros and cons of taking a meeting with you instead of a brisk click.

Objections are where the cold call really begins. And that's what's up next. So congratulations, you've completed Section 1. But before you move on, we've got some homework for you to make sure that it really sticks.

Top 4 Actionable Takeaways from Chapter 2

- **No Value Propositions.** Buzzwords make you sound like a telemarketer, and benefits fall flat without the context of a problem.

- **Triggering Problem.** Instead, lead with a problem so specific that it triggers your prospect and reminds them of a painful memory.

- **One-Sentence Solution**. If you get the problem right, all you need is one sentence to explain your solution (we do X so that the problem goes away).

- **Interest-Based CTA**. Validate their interest before you ask for the meeting, using softening language, no-based questions, and mini push-aways.

CHAPTER 2 HOMEWORK: BUILD YOUR COLD CALL SCRIPT

This will be an exercise in academic theory if you do not put this into practice and make it your own. Below, you will find a beautiful gift from Nick and me …

A blank table.

Scan the QR below and write your opener and problem proposition in the table below.

Then, you guessed it. Practice it 100 times on the streets of San Francisco (or wherever).

Tailored Permission Opener	
Lead with Context	
Own the Cold Call	
Ask for Permission	
Heard The Name Tossed Around Opener	
Lead with Context	
Then Intro Yourself	
Heard the Name?	
Problem Proposition	
Triggering Problem	
One-Sentence Solution	
Interest-Based CTA	

Section 1 Pro Tip: Read and Listen for Retention

Congratulations, you've made it through the first section of the book. When I'm really enjoying a book, I'll usually start listening to the audiobook around Chapter 2 to really get things to sink in.

There's something about listening *and* reading that helps me retain the concepts—especially with something like cold calling where tone is so important. Plus, you'll get a second pass through the content.

If you're enjoying the read, you might consider listening, too. Scan the QR code below or find it wherever you get your audiobooks.

Get the Audiobook

THE REST OF THE CALL

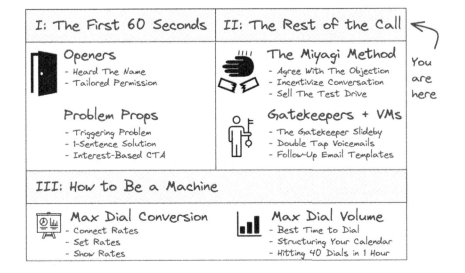

Now that you know how to nail the first 60 seconds of your cold call, Section 2 covers *everything else* that can happen on a cold call.

Chapter 3 covers how to handle objections like Mr. Miyagi. We'll break down 3 steps you can use to handle *any* objection after the first 60 seconds.

Chapter 4 covers 18 common objections and how to handle them. We'll apply the Mr. Miyagi Method to the 18 most common objections and leave you with talk tracks for each.

Chapter 5 covers gatekeepers and voicemails. In other words, what to do when you can't get to your first 60 seconds at all.

There are two full chapters dedicated to objections—the single hardest part of cold calling.

I wish the entire cold call was as easy as the first 60 seconds. Your opener and problem proposition are largely static, but you have no idea what will come next …

- *I'm not interested.*
- *Where'd you get my number!?*
- *I'm using this [random niche competitor you've never heard of].*

In a matter of seconds, you need to blunt their knee-jerk reaction, mentally process the objection, and say something moderately intelligent to get them talking for 30 more seconds.

Put on your white belt, young grasshopper. It is time to learn the way of Mr. Miyagi.

WATAHHHHHH!!!!

HOW TO HANDLE OBJECTIONS LIKE MR. MIYAGI

Agenda
• Why most objections aren't actually objections
• The three steps to handle any objection like Mr. Miyagi
• When and how to book the meeting

 **I**lied to a salesperson just last week.

Last weekend, I decided I was going to spend a quiet afternoon posted up at a coffee shop to make some progress writing this book.

20 minutes into my writing session, just as I was starting to pick up some steam, I was interrupted mid-paragraph by a young man clearing his throat to get my attention:

"Erm, excuse me, sir?"

I looked up from my laptop to see an overly friendly college student donned in a bright orange ASPCA vest grinning at me. Uh-oh, here comes the sales pitch.

"Sir, do you happen to love animals?"

Now, under normal circumstances, I don't know anyone who'd say, "No, I don't love animals." I certainly consider myself an animal lover, and I've actually donated to animal rescue causes in the past.

But I was right in the middle of writing this book, and he completely interrupted me in the flow of things. I wanted to make this salesperson go away so I could get back to writing, so I said the first thing I could think of to get him to scram:

"Nope, I don't!"

My real objection was to his interruption, not to his cause. I knew if I told him the truth (I love animals), it would only prolong the interruption, and the next thing you'd know, I'd be dealing with a sales pitch to sign a petition or make a donation when I just wanted to get back to writing.

This is exactly what most prospects are doing when they give *you* an objection too. They're reacting to the interruption, and it has nothing to do with your pitch.

Most Objections Aren't Really Objections

Visual evidence that my objection was fake.

Cold calling might be part of *your* job, but for your prospect, it's an entirely unwelcome interruption to their day.

The jarring interruption from a stranger sends your prospect into a fight-or-flight state where they're searching for the first excuse they can find to make you go away.

The first objection is almost always a knee-jerk reaction, not their real objection. They're not actually considering the pros and cons of anything you're trying to sell them. They're just telling you that they don't like animals so that you go away.

On a cold call, dismissive objections are the same thing: *I'm not interested, call me in 6 months,* or *send me some information* aren't real objections. They're reactions to the interruption.

This is where most sellers screw up. They try to "handle" those objections by pressuring the prospect with logic. They hurl their pitch at the prospect, reiterate the value of their product, or push for the meeting … but this only makes them push away *more.*

You can't overcome emotion with logic. You need to disarm the emotional reaction *first.* You need to move them from reacting to listening. To do that, you need some sort of pattern break that gets them to realize you're an actual human capable of having a conversation.

That's why the first step of the Mr. Miyagi method is to disarm their reaction by agreeing with the objection.

There's nothing more disarming than agreeing with their objection. When they snap, "I've got it taken care of," they're expecting you to do what every other telemarketer does. Pitch.

Instead, you're gonna say, "Yeah, it probably doesn't make sense for you to switch."

And they're gonna think, *Wait … you're not gonna try to sell me?*

It's like they tried to sit in a chair, and you pulled it out from underneath them. It feels really stupid to keep fighting someone who's not trying to fight back.

Now they'll be far more likely to give you the real reason behind their objection, at which point we can start to logically overcome it.

This is the crux of the Mr. Miyagi method. We're not going to fight objections. We're going to absorb the momentum of the reaction by agreeing with them first.

Introduction to the Mr. Miyagi Method

| Agree With The Objection | Incentivize Conversation | Sell The Test Drive |

In the movie *Karate Kid*, Mr. Miyagi doesn't counter enemy punches right away. Instead, he waxes them on and off. He redirects the momentum of the punch entirely to dispel the conflict.

That's how we're going to approach objections. In the Dojo of Mondo Miyagi-Do, there are 3 steps to handling any objection in the world. Let's use the objection "I have no budget" as an example.

Step 1—Agree with the objection. Remove all the pressure of the sale to disarm the reaction:

I hear ya. Nowadays, it's hard enough to keep your budget, let alone add something new.

Step 2—Incentivize conversation. People will resist recommendations until they feel like you understand their situation. If you can get them talking, you allow them to air out their concerns, which makes them far more likely to hear you out in return. But it's not easy to get a stranger talking, so we'll provide an incentive … no more cold calls:

Just so no one calls you again, is it that you're out of budget for this fiscal year or you get put through the wringer every time you try to buy something?

Step 3—Sell the test drive. Selling the product now will only reapply the pressure you just worked hard to remove. Instead, sell the test drive—what they will get out of the meeting—even if they never buy the car.

I get it. Hey, you're probably not gonna buy this thing now. But if budget ever frees up, the people who get it at least have a directional sense of what they'd want. Open to taking a look, so you at least know what's out there?

That's your white belt lesson. Let's break it down so you can get your black belt.

Step 1—Agree With the Objection

As Nick said earlier, it feels really stupid to fight someone who's not fighting back. When you agree with the objection, your prospect wakes up because it's a complete pattern break from every other telemarketer who'd normally pitch.

But you can't just say … *you're right!* You need to agree with their *specific* objection for it to be believable. Here's what that looks like for a few common objections:

- **Not Interested**. Ah, my bad. You probably would've reached out to us if you needed help.

- **No Budget.** I hear ya. Nowadays, it's hard enough to keep something that's in the budget, let alone ask for something new.
- **Competitor.** I should've assumed you'd be all set. Honestly, most of the time, it doesn't make sense to switch when you've got something in place.

Notice, it's helpful to lead with a "micro agree" statement that can apply to *any* objection while you think of the best way to handle the *specific* objection. That could be:

- I totally get that, _____
- I completely understand, _____
- That one's on me, _____
- I should've assumed you'd be all set, _____

Once you're done agreeing with the full objection, it's still too early to re-propose a meeting. We need to turn the reaction into a conversation in step 2.

Step 2—Incentivize Conversation

It's a classic telemarketer move to agree with the objection (*I should've assumed you'd be all set*) and then immediately reapply the pressure (*but*

what other customers have found is ...). This erodes all trust and tells your prospect that any information they give you will be immediately met with a counter-pitch.

So before you "handle" the objection, it's critical to get them talking for 3 reasons:

Reason #1) They feel understood. Think about the last time someone gave you unsolicited advice, and you resisted it. Usually, it's because they told you what to do without taking the time to understand why you made certain decisions on your own *first*.

Reason #2) You increase talk time. It takes time to separate yourself from the initial "telemarketer" interruption and demonstrate that you're able to hold an intelligent conversation. For this reason (and the fact that a prospect usually has multiple objections), Gong data validates that the longer the conversation goes, the more likely you are to book the meeting:

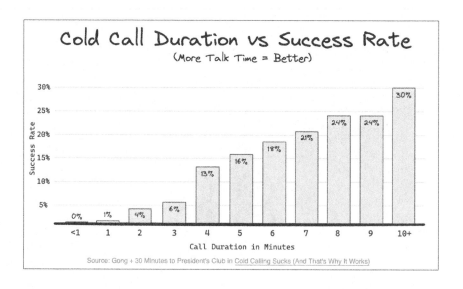

Reason #3) They reveal missing information. They will often reveal the real objection or share more about the existing objection so you can handle it more effectively.

The way you do this is by asking a question that encourages them to pile onto the objection *even more*. You need to jump on the same side of the objection and have them push it even further for them to truly feel heard.

The problem is most prospects won't share much about their business with a complete stranger. If you ask, "What tool are you on?" or "When will budget clear up?" they'll clam up.

Provide an incentive for them to share more … No more cold calls! The reality is that no one wants to be cold called again. Tell them that the reason you're seeking to understand the objection is so that you *really know* they're not worth calling.

Here's how that plays out:

- **Not Interested.** Just so no one reaches out again, is it that you've got something in place, you're doing it yourself, or you just hate getting cold calls?
- **No Budget.** Just so no one reaches out again, is it that there's no budget for this cycle, or you get put through the wringer any time you try to spend it?
- **Competitor.** Just so no one reaches out again, are you sponsoring Sales Goon, Commission Carl, or someone else?

> ## Pro Tip: Use Multiple Choice
>
> Add multiple-choice to your questions, and they'll be far more likely to answer. When you lay out the 2–3 potential situations they could be in, you establish credibility as an industry insider and make it easy for them to pick one.

Agreeing and incentivizing conversation are the most critical steps in the Miyagi Method. When combined, they create a no-pressure sale zone that makes them far more likely to agree to a test drive in step 3.

Step 3—Sell the Test Drive

Do not fight the objection.

You're not going to convince them that your product is better than the competition or that they can *find* budget … on a cold call.

But you *can* convince them to take a look. That's when you address those concerns.

Most people have zero intention of buying a Tesla, but they *do* want to know what it feels like to drive one. Tesla knows they're expensive.

But they also know that if they get you into the car, you're going to feel like you're in a rocket ship.

Exhibit A: Prospect converted by the test drive

And that's your job: get them in the car.

If you get them in the car, you will have all the time in the world to ask more about their current car, what sucks about it, and how you can make it better.

You sell the test drive by answering this question: **Why would they want to take a meeting with you … even if they don't buy?**

For example, here's how you sell the test drive for those same 3 objections:

1. **Not Interested** (due to an in-house solution). You probably won't outgrow your solution for a while. But would you be opposed to taking a look, and if nothing else you might get some ideas to add to your own process?

2. **No Budget**. Hey, you're probably not gonna buy this thing now. But if budget ever frees up, the people who get it at least have a directional sense of what they'd want. Open to taking a look, and if nothing else you can add it to your wishlist?

3. **Competitor**. Honestly, it rarely makes sense to replace Sales Goon, but we've had a few customers switch due to X, Y, and Z. Would you be completely against taking a look, if for no other reason than to get a sense of the tradeoffs?

Notice the use of **mini push-aways** before we sell the test drive:

- "You're probably not gonna buy this."
- "My guess is you're all set."
- "I don't think you'll make the switch now."

I know it feels counterintuitive, but they're far more likely to *try* a test drive if they feel you're not going to hard-pressure them to *buy* the car.

White Belt Tip: Start With the Generic Test Drive

If you can't think of something specific, you can always fall back on the generic test drive: "My guess is you're not gonna buy this, but open to taking a look, not for now, but so you know what's out there?"

It still works wonders. Once you get more comfortable, get more specific.

Full Mr. Miyagi Example (With Tone)

Throughout the entire Miyagi Method, you can say all the right things, but the wrong tone can actually escalate the conflict of the first objection. If you come off as timid, rushed, or rattled, your prospect will categorize you as someone who's junior and has nothing to offer them.

Let's put it all together and nail the delivery. Using the same *no-budget* example, listen closely to the tone of this conversation by scanning the QR below:

Prospect: Sorry, we don't have any budget.

You (Agree): I hear ya. Nowadays, it's hard enough to keep your budget, let alone add something new.

You (Incentivize): Just so no one calls you again, is it that there's no budget for this cycle or that any spend whatsoever requires you to do a triple backflip?

Prospect: It's a bit of both, to be frank. We're really tight right now.

You (Test Drive): I get it. Hey, you're probably not gonna buy this thing now.

But if budget ever frees up, the people who get it at least have a *directional* sense of what they'd want.

Open to taking a look, so you at least know what's out there?

Listen for the following cues:

First, you have to slow it down, especially upon hearing the objection. Most sellers speed up, stammer, and sweat when they hear *I'm not interested* or *I'm in a meeting*. The moment you speed up and try to jam in *b-b-but could I get 30 seconds to tell you why I c-called* … it's too late.

When you let them dictate the pace of your speech, they see you in a light of inferiority. But if you slow down and look at them sorta funny with a raised eyebrow … you come off as a peer who expects the same level of respect, and *they'll* feel like the jerk.

Moreover, you give yourself time to think when you slow down. You stutter and use filler words when your mouth is moving faster than your mind. Let your brain load.

The Most Interesting Man in the World never speaks quickly.

I literally tell myself "pause, slow down" before handling an objection (even when recording the conversation above). You *know* the objection is coming. Wait a full two seconds, use the "Micro-Agree" to buy yourself time, then proceed *slower than you think you need to* as if someone was playing your voice on 0.5x speed.

To demonstrate how long you can pause and how slow you can really go, listen to this *super slow* agree version. Honestly, I might like it even more than the original:

Super Slow Agree Version

Second, laugh when you get an objection to show that you're comfortable, like a peer. Especially for nasty objections, make them realize that *they're* the ones being silly for throwing a temper tantrum. Laughing rebalances the power dynamic and often gets them to realize, *Okay, maybe I was a bit of a jerk there.*

Third, shrug when you're selling the test drive. Your tone needs to sound like it's *really* a no-pressure test drive. Think, *Hey, wanna check it out just for kicks?*

If you sound overly eager, they're gonna imagine the high-pressure mall kiosk salesman even if you *claim* that it's a no-pressure test drive.

Chain Objection Handling

The good news: You have everything you need to navigate any *single* objection in the world.

The bad news: It's rarely enough to handle just one objection.

Gong data shows that the median *successful* call duration is 4.8 minutes, which means you'll need to handle a minimum of two objections to land the meeting.

You've gotta be ready to do some *Chain Objection Handling*, where you handle multiple objections before you land the meeting.

Here's how it often plays out …

- **You give your problem proposition and a prospect barks that they're all set.** So you agree with the objection and ask if it's because they're handling things in house, using a competitor, or simply hate getting cold called.

- **Now they reveal that they're using a competitor.** You fall back on the Miyagi framework again, and sell the test drive by offering to share why other customers switched so that they know what's out there.

- **Now they're interested, but their current contract doesn't end for 6 months.** Miyagi again! Sell the test drive by giving them options today that might help them negotiate their upcoming renewal in 6 months.

Eventually, you'll feel your prospect open up and ask you questions about your offering. That's when it's time for you to book the meeting.

*   *   *

Alrighty, your mind is probably in a cold calling jujitsu pretzel, and you're cycling through the dozens of objections you've received in your life and trying to figure out how to apply the 3 steps to each. Don't worry, we have you covered.

Take a deep breath and try to nail *one* objection. Then get ready because we're going to show you how to handle the 18 most common objections step-by-step in the next chapter.

Top 4 Actionable Takeaways from Chapter 3

- **Agree with the objection** to disarm their defense mechanism.
- **Incentivize conversation** by asking for the real reason behind their objection so that you know they're not worth calling again.
- **Sell the test drive** by offering something of value even if they don't buy.
- **Slow down and laugh** to show them you're comfortable, like a peer.

CHAPTER 3 HOMEWORK:
AGREE AND INCENTIVIZE 100 TIMES

They see a tourist trolley. You see a karate dojo.

Look at that, we're back to practicing on our morning commute. Come on, you'd never practice waxing a punch on and off ... *in the karate tournament*.

The most crucial (and difficult) parts of the Mr. Miyagi Method are the first two steps. Within a matter of seconds, you need to figure out how to agree with the objection in a way that's believable and ask a semi-intelligent question.

This is your practice plan:

- Pick your top 4 objections.
- Agree and incentivize each objection 25 times on your next commute.
- Bonus points if you role-play each objection 5 times with a peer or your manager (that should take you under 30 minutes if you're efficient).

I explicitly recommend doing this *before* you read the 18 objection talk tracks in the next chapter. This will force you to think critically through each objection so that you can master *any* objection, whether or not you have a script.

On that note … let's talk about scripts before we dive in.

DISCLAIMER BEFORE CHAPTER 4:
DO NOT MEMORIZE SCRIPTS

If you master the three steps of the Miyagi Method, you will never have to memorize a script.

When you recite a script word-for-word:

- **Your tone will show it**: You will sound rigid (like a telemarketer).

- **They'll know you're not listening**: Your talk tracks will be just *slightly off* if there's any nuance in the objection, which shows them you weren't actually listening.

- **You'll get stuck**: Even if you memorize these 18 objections, you'll encounter a 19th. Moreover, you can't memorize the 100+ if-this-then-that responses that will follow.

So, we debated this chapter at length. Why in the world would we include talk tracks at all?

We decided to include them for one purpose. To make it real.

Here are our 3 ground rules for this chapter:

1. **Focus less on the words and more on the delivery**. We gave you lots of examples of how to use humor and tone so that you can build your own style.

2. **Use this chapter as a reference guide**. Don't try to remember everything on the first go. Pick 1–2 objections to master, then revisit this chapter when a new one stumps you.

3. **Practice, then reveal**. Practice each objection out loud, *then* read the talk track. If you said something that was directionally similar, congratulations because …

You didn't need the script.

18 OBJECTIONS AND HOW TO HANDLE THEM

Agenda
• Dismissive Objections (i.e., not interested, call me in 6 months)
• Situational Objections (i.e., no budget, no bandwidth)
• Existing Solution Objections (i.e., competitors, in-house solutions)

Now that you have the framework to handle any objection in the world, your goal is to apply that framework as specifically as possible to each objection you hear.

But this is easier said than done when there are dozens of objections, so it's often helpful to think of objections in buckets where you know the strategy for each category. Knowing the strategy for each category of objection will get you 50% of the way there, then your listening skills and practice will take you the rest of the way.

There are 3 categories of objections, in order of how often they appear per Gong Data:

1. **49.5% are Dismissive Objections:** Brush-offs such as *not interested, I'm in a meeting, call me in 6 months,* and *where'd you get my number?* (a fan favorite)

2. **42.6% are Situational Objections:** When their situation and your product don't line up, such as *no budget, too expensive, no bandwidth or resources, or product objections.*

3. **7.9% are Existing Solution Objections:** Alternatives to your product, such as *in-house solutions, competitors, and being stuck in a contract.*

As expected, nearly 50% of objections will be dismissive swats (aka: knee-jerk reactions). And, honestly, most situational objections are knee-jerk reactions too. Even people who have "no bandwidth" can find time to solve a problem that's lighting their hair on fire.

For each category, we'll break down the high-level approach, then give example talk tracks for the 18 most common objections that you'll encounter. Remember, you can either scan the QR codes or go to 30mpc.com/guide to access all the talk tracks, data charts, and drawings in one place.

Here's the list of the 18 common objections by category:

Dismissive Objections	1. Not interested
	2. Call me in 6 months
	3. Send me some information
	4. Not my responsibility
	5. Where'd you get my number!?
	6. I'm in a meeting
	7. Is this a cold call?
	8. I thought you were someone else
	9. *hang up*

Situational Objections	1. Too expensive
	2. No budget
	3. No resources/bandwidth
	4. We need to hire someone first
	5. Product fit (not made for us)
Existing Solution Objections	1. We do it in-house
	2. Competitor (known)
	3. Competitor (unknown)
	4. Stuck in a contract

The top 5 most common objections actually account for 74% of all objections. If you master these, you'll be covered 3 out of 4 times, which is pretty good:

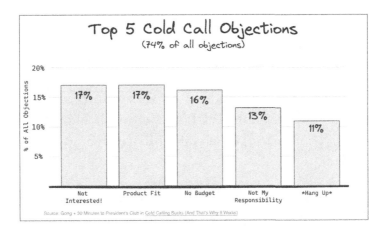

That said, these can vary greatly by industry, so here's how you can decide which objections are most important for you:

- Build your base by learning the approach for each category.
- Start with the top objections *you* receive at your company.
- Move to the top 5 most common objections above.
- Cover the rest

You have your blue belt. Let's earn that black belt.

Dismissive Objections Overview

 Dismissive objections are the most common knee-jerk reactions to a cold call. They're telling you *I don't like animals* in the form of *I'm not interested* or *call me in 6 months*.

The hardest part about dismissive objections is that they're not real objections. You have nothing to work with because you have no idea *why* they aren't interested or *why* you should call back in 6 months. So, you have to agree and incentivize them to share the real objection first.

These can also escalate into some of the most abrasive objections of them all. It's one thing to reason with someone who says *I'm not interested*. It's another thing to reason with an irate old man yelling, "Is this a cold call!?"

Your natural reaction will be to stammer, apologize, and scurry away. Do the opposite.

Dispel the tension with "Disarmingly Blunt" transparency and humor. The more ridiculous their reaction, the more ridiculous your *opposite* counter-reaction should be:

If someone says ...	You say ...
Is this a cold call!?	Yes, and I'm sorry because it's going so, so poorly ...
I'm in a meeting!!	Oh, shoot! Well, if you want, you can put me on speaker to publicly apologize to the group, and I can really bomb on this one.
Where'd you get my phone number!?	It's a contact database called Banana Leads. It sounds like I really ruined your day here, so I'd be happy to send you a screenshot of what they have on file so you know what's out there.

It's really hard to get mad at someone who's leaning *into* the misery of the confrontation or being far *more* transparent than they could've expected by sharing a screenshot of your contact database. Again, it's like you're pulling the chair out from underneath them.

Do it right, and the prospect should wake up and realize there's a human on the other line. And at that point, you can ask a question that draws out an *actual* objection.

Let's dive in.

1) Dismissive Objection: Not Interested

Not interested is the most common objection in the world. It's also the most fake objection in the world. They're not actually contemplating your product; they're just annoyed and trying to give you as little information as they can to justify a brisk hang-up.

Be disarmingly blunt and agree with this one really hard to wake them up. Blame it on your pitch and call out the fact that they hate getting cold calls, so they loosen up a bit. From there, use that to get them to *actually* think about why they're not interested:

Prospect: I'm not interested.	
You (Agree): Shoot, my bad Nick. I guess either my pitch was really crummy, or you would've reached out to *us* if you were interested.	*Guilt to prevent a quick hang-up*
You (Incentivize): Just so no one calls you again, could you be brutally honest with me …	
Is it that you've got a solution, you're not thinking about this problem at all, or you just hate getting cold calls? And it's okay if it's #3!	*Disarmingly blunt*
Prospect: We're already working with Sales Goon.	*The real objection!*
From here, run Miyagi again (see objection #16: competitor)	

You'll notice we didn't sell the test drive because we didn't have the real objection.

Once you get the real objection (in this case, a competitor), run the full Miyagi Method from the top *again* and finish it off with the test drive.

2) Dismissive Objection: Call Me in 6 Months

Sure, that meeting's *definitely* coming your way in 6 months. Then 9 months. Then 12 months. Next thing you know, your prospect is in the witness protection program. They're nowhere to be found.

A prospect usually says *call me in 6 months* when they're too nice to say *I'm not interested.* So use multiple-choice to figure out if there's a real reason to call back or if they're just "busy."

If there is a real reason, sell the test drive today so the decision is easier later:

Prospect: Open to it, but not now. Mind calling in 6 months?	
You (Agree): Totally makes sense. I guess if you were ready now, you would've reached out to us.	
You (Incentivize): Just so I don't sound like a goon when I call back, was there something specific happening in 6 months or are you just swamped?	*Multiple-choice*
Prospect: We're hiring a new CMO and nothing's changing until then.	*Ah, real reason.*
You (Test Drive): Yeah, I wouldn't wanna make any big decisions before then either.	*Push-away.*

Hey, crazy idea. I know you're not gonna buy this now, but oftentimes a CMO comes in and wants to see what tools are at their disposal.

Push-away again.

If nothing else, would you be opposed to taking a look so that you can give her a sense of her options when she arrives?

AKA: Look good in front of the new boss

But 9 out of 10 times, there's no real reason. They're just "busy." So if that's the case *or* they still say no to the test drive, we'll use my favorite disarmingly blunt line to call it out in the next objection (and that line works perfectly here too).

3) Dismissive Objection: Send Me Some Information

Call me in 6 months and send me some information are very similar objections. No one *actually* wants to read your generic marketing materials; they're just too nice to reject you. Instead, be disarmingly blunt and call it out:

Prospect: Thanks; send me some information, and I'll take a look.	
You (Agree): Oh, for sure. I'd wanna digest it all first too.	
You (Incentivize): Just so I don't clutter your inbox, was there a specific question you had in mind or just a general overview?	*Multiple-choice*
Prospect: Just a general overview.	*AKA: Not interested*
You (Test Drive): Ha ha, I'm the king of "this meeting should've been an email" too. But I'll be honest: those PDFs aren't gonna be relevant at all … and you'll *know* if this is a fit in the first 15 minutes. Opposed to taking a look, and if it's not a fit, I can give you 15 back?"	*Disarmingly blunt*
Prospect: No, no, I'd really prefer some information.	*Give them control*
You (Permission): Okay, waving my white flag! Before I go, mind if I ask you a brutally honest question?	*Use permission for hard questions*

Prospect: Sure.	
You (Disarmingly Blunt) When folks tell me to send them some info, they're just too nice to tell me to go away. Is that what's happening?	*Call them out in compliments.*
Prospect: No, of course not! I promise I'll at least take a look.	
You (The Dart): Okay, here's our deal. I'll send you the info, call out *exactly* what's relevant to you, and send a placeholder invite for next week. If you don't like it, you can just decline the invite. Fair?	*I put time into my follow-up, you agree to read it*

When you call out the lie, get them to stand by it, and *then* put even more work into your follow-up to create goodwill … they're far more likely to accept the placeholder meeting.

4) Dismissive Objection: Not My Responsibility

There are one of two possibilities. They're either the right person (and they're lying), or they're actually the wrong person. Regardless, the approach is the same.

Drop the name and title of the person you think *should* be responsible for evaluating your product. If they were lying, they'll fess up with the real objection because they don't want you to cold call their colleague. From there, run Miyagi again on that objection.

If they're *not* the right person, your goal is to get a referral instead of a test drive. I find that it's very unlikely that *they'll* make the referral because you're a complete stranger. Instead, I ask for permission to mention their name when *I* reach out to their colleague:

Prospect: Yeah, that's not my responsibility.	
You (Agree): Ah, my bad. It's funny; this kind of thing usually either lives with you as the Head of Content or with your Head of Demand Generation. Guess I was wrong here.	*Know the personas that buy your thing*
You (Incentivize): Just so I don't bug the wrong person, is this in Jane's court? (Their Head of Demand Generation)	*I'm calling her next*
Prospect: Yeah, Jane would be the one.	
You (Permission): Could I ask you for an extremely unreasonable favor from a complete stranger?	*Use permission for big asks.*

Prospect: Sure.	
You (Referral): I was gonna send her a note after this. Mind if I let her know we spoke?	*Note: I was already gonna reach out*

When you make it clear you were gonna reach out to the other prospect anyway, they're more likely to agree to the name drop. From here, I'll usually **write a new email to the referral with the subject line:** *Spoke with Nick*. You'll get a reply.

Note on Objections 5–9: "Pre-Pitch" Dismissive Objections

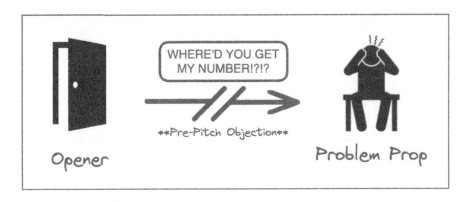

There are a few dismissive objections that often happen right after your cold call opener *before* you can even deliver your problem proposition. These include:

- Where'd you get my number!?
- I'm in a meeting.
- Is this a cold call?
- I thought you were someone else.
- *hang up*

For pre-pitch objections, your goal is *not* to surface the real objection or sell the test drive because they literally have no idea what you do.

Your goal is to get *back* to your problem proposition by agreeing, incentivizing, and pivoting back to your permission-based opener.

Let's walk through how to do this for the next 5.

Warning: These are the nastiest objections of all. Get ready to be disarmingly blunt in return.

5) Pre-Pitch Dismissive Objection: Where'd You Get My Number!?

Remember, agree hard and be disarmingly blunt. Many reps will sweat, stammer, and hesitate to share how they found the number (as if contact databases were a hidden secret).

Instead, be disarmingly blunt by explicitly sharing the name of the tool *and* offering to screenshot their entry in the database. Your prospect is clearly surprised and pissed off. But you can pattern break by being even more transparent than they expected you to be:

Prospect (Pre-Pitch): Where'd you get my phone number!?	
You (Agree): Oh shoot! It's a contact database called Banana Leads.	*Disarmingly blunt*
It sounds like I really ruined your day here, so I'd be happy to send you a screenshot of what they have on file so you know what's out there.	*Disarmingly blunt*
Prospect: Well … no that's fine, I don't need that.	
You (Incentivize): Look, I don't love making these calls, and I know you don't love getting them. But I actually prepared for this one.	*Disarmingly blunt*
Just so no one calls you again, could I tell you why I called you *specifically*, then you can hang up on me from there?	*Permission*

From here, they'll usually ease off the gas because you're double incentivizing them by not only offering to make this the last cold call they get from you but perhaps the last cold call they get from anyone with this contact list.

6) Pre-Pitch Dismissive Objection: I'm in a Meeting!

This one frankly pisses me off. No one is answering their phone in a meeting, and if they were, it clearly wasn't important. It's the most BS swat of them all, so I prefer to match the ridiculousness of the objection with a laughably unreasonable ask to put me on speakerphone.

From there, many sellers make the mistake of offering to call back at another time, at which point your prospect enters the witness protection program and never answers your call again.

Instead, give them two options: a calendar invite for later or a conversation now:

Prospect (Pre-Pitch): I'm literally in a meeting.	*Liar*
You (Agree): Oh shoot! Well, if you want, you can put me on speaker to publicly apologize to the group, and I can really bomb on this one.	*Disarmingly blunt*
Prospect: No, no … what's this about?	
You (Incentivize): But actually, I'd *hate* to interrupt you again.	
Would you rather have me send a hold to call you back at the top of the hour or briefly tell you why I called now so I don't bug ya again?	*Meet later or get it over with?*

The calendar invite sounds really unattractive because now they're agreeing to a *second* cold call, and frankly, they don't want random invites from a stranger.

For everyone else who wants the callback, send the invite. Sure, maybe they'll decline it. But a 50-50 shot at a calendar invite is better than calling back to find out they blocked your number.

Plus, you can attach a personalized video or a thoughtful note to the invitation to build some goodwill and increase the chances that it sticks.

7) Pre-Pitch Dismissive Objection: Is This a Cold Call!?

This is almost always an irate old man in shock that he's being cold called. If you freak out, stammer, and sweat, you're only justifying his tantrum, and you're gonna get bulldozed.

Be the opposite of irate and unreasonable so *they* feel ridiculous for reacting like a child.

Call out the fact that the call is going horribly, and both of you aren't enjoying this. Give them the right to slam the door in your face, and they'll realize they're completely out of line:

Prospect (After Your Opener): Is this a cold call!?	
You (Agree): Yes, and it's going so, so badly.	*Disarmingly blunt*
Look, I know you probably hate getting cold calls. I honestly don't like making them either, but I took some time to research you personally because everyone hates telemarketers.	*Disarmingly blunt*
You (Incentivize): Just so no one from my team ruins your day again, could I tell you why I called, and, if nothing else, you can hang up on me then if it's really not a fit?	*Permission*

If you approached this prospect at a conference with some really thoughtful things you knew about them, there's no way they'd chew you out on the public floor. **Recreate the face-to-face interaction through your words, and they'll feel like a total jerk for piling on more.**

The only reason they're doing this is because it's a cold call.

8) Pre-Pitch Dismissive Objection: I thought you were someone else.

Okay, imagine this. You're waiting for your good friend Nick to show up at your house. The snacks are ready. The music is bumping. You're having a jolly old time.

Ding-dong! You rush to the door, champagne glass in hand.

"Ayyyyy! Come on i-i–..." *Oh ... the solar panel guy.*

"Wanna save on your Prius charging bill?"

When it gets awkward, *lean into it*. If you act awkward, you're just a lingering annoyance. But crack a good joke, and you'll usually get a shot on goal like this:

Prospect (After Your Opener): I thought you were someone else.	
You (Agree): Well, I can change my tone of voice and pretend to be someone different if you'd like!	*Disarmingly blunt*
But actually, I hate it when I'm waiting for a call, then I pick up and someone's trying to sell me SiriusXM radio.	
You (Incentivize): I'd hate to do this to you *twice*.	
Could I just tell you why I called you, and I promise if that person calls you back, you can hang up on the spot?	*Give them the out*

It's critical when you pivot back to your permission-based opener, you let them know that they can hang up if that person calls back. Otherwise, they won't give you permission because they're worried about missing the callback.

Notice the pattern with these last few. Make a joke that almost seems more extreme than the objection itself. Ask for permission using an incentive (just so we don't interrupt you again).

And just as we were getting that pattern down, this last one is a change-up. Silence.

9) Pre-Pitch Dismissive Objection: *Hang Up*

Many people say you should immediately call back a prospect who just hung up and say something like, "I think we got disconnected."

The success rate with this approach is basically zero. You both know they hung up, and you're only going to frustrate them more by calling back immediately and acting dumb.

Instead, make a note of these 3 things when someone hangs up: The call date, the call time, and the *exact* words they said before hanging up. Move on to your next dial for now.

Call back a week later and use those 3 things as context in your tailored permission opener:

Prospect (Pre-Pitch): I can't talk now; I'm crazy busy preparing for a big meeting. *hang up*	
One Week Later	
You (Context): Emma, you and I last spoke on October 19th around 2:30 in the afternoon. At the time, you couldn't talk because you were crazy busy preparing for a big meeting, and you admittedly hung up on me.	*Date & Time* *Guilt*
You (Own the Cold Call): I know I was an interruption, and I guess I'm interrupting you now ... but I promise I prepped for this one, and I'm calling you for a reason.	*Guilt x 2*
You (Permission): Could I at least tell you why I called you back, and then you can totally hang up on me from there?	*Guilt x 3*

When you cite the exact date, time, and words the prospect said ... *and* restate what you know about them, you get their attention. You recreate the moment when they hung up on an actual human being who was really trying to have a thoughtful conversation. They'll feel like a jerk.

This also shows that you're professionally persistent. Not because they're dial number 472, but because there's something we saw about them that made us call again.

If they hang up again, try the same approach on a different channel (Email, LinkedIn)—we'll cover some approaches for that at the end of the next chapter.

Situational Objections Overview

In 2015, I left Los Angeles to move to San Francisco and work in tech.

For 8 years straight, whenever I visited home, my mom would ask me to clean out my childhood closet. Everything from 3rd grade yearbooks to wrestling trophies to Pokemon Cards lived in there.

It was a minor annoyance for both of us. It was an annoyance to visit home after working 60-hour weeks as a VP of Sales, only to have my mom tell me to clean my room.

And it was an annoyance for her to see a poorly utilized closet filled with Pokemon Cards now owned by a 31-year-old.

No way Mom was throwing away this gold.

But it was not *so* annoying to either of us that we *really* wanted to do anything about it. Because if it was, *I* would have cleared out the closet, or *she* would've thrown away my 1998 Holographic Blastoise along with the rest of my collection.

We both implicitly agreed that the benefits of a clean closet were not greater than the big transition pain of the closet overhaul.

This is what a prospect feels when you ask them to consider a new product.

Buying products means an investment of time, money, and people. Even if they see the benefits, they imagine *all* the work they'll have to do to realize them: begging for budget, assigning someone to manage the project, burning political capital if it doesn't work.

The cost of the *transition* outweighs the benefits of the product. So you have to remove all the pressure of *buying* the car until you get them so excited that they realize it's worth it.

You do that with the test drive. Once they're in the car, we can blow their mind with the drive, explain how easy it is to finance the car, and let them drive it off the lot today.

But not on a cold call. Get them in the car.

(P.S. Last year, I did in fact clean up my childhood closet for Mom.)

10) Situational Objection: No Budget

Prospects rarely have spare dollars waiting to be spent. But this is a common situational objection because asking for money is painful. They have to risk political capital, put together ROI cases, and even replace existing tools. Acknowledge this when you agree.

Another factor is that budgets work in cycles. Use multiple-choice to determine if it's a timing issue (i.e., new budget will be released) or a value issue (you'll have to fight to create budget).

Regardless of their response, remove the pressure of the purchase entirely. Instead, give them a way to win more funds for their team, which is a test drive that everyone wants:

Prospect: Sorry, we don't have any budget.	
You (Agree): I hear ya. Nowadays, it's hard enough to keep your budget, let alone add something new.	
You (Incentivize) Just so no one calls you again, is it that there's no budget for this cycle or that any spend requires you to do a triple backflip?	*Tells us if it's a timing or value issue*
Prospect: It's a bit of both, to be frank. We're really tight right now.	
You (Test Drive): I get it. Hey, you're probably not gonna buy this thing now.	*Mini push-away*

But if budget ever frees up, the people who get it at least have a directional sense of what's on their wishlist. Open to taking a look, so you at least know what's out there?	*Don't lose your shot to buy something*

This is a good example of a mini push-away statement in action. Use them a lot with situational objections. Unlike dismissive objections, they're not fighting the interruption *as much* as they're fighting the thought of buying something.

11) Situational Objection: Too Expensive

This one is really similar to no budget, except it's externally aimed at your product instead of internally aimed at their approval process.

One of two things is true: either the past rep couldn't sell the value, or this prospect really is freaking cheap and got sticker shock. So, use multiple-choice to figure that out.

Regardless, you're not going to convince them that it's worth the price on the call. So explain that there's flexibility on price without locking yourself into a discount. That's your test drive:

Prospect: Your product's way too expensive.	
You (Agree): Oh, that's interesting. Look, we're never the cheapest, but we're also never astronomically expensive.	
You (Incentivize): If you don't mind me asking, just so no one calls again, was it the sheer dollar amount or the fact that you didn't see enough value for the price?	*Sticker shock or value issue?*
Prospect: It looked cool, but we're paying around $12k per year now and couldn't justify paying $20k with you.	*There's interest.*
You (Test Drive): Look, not crazy far off. But we can skinny this down or beef it up depending on what you need.	*Allude to flexibility*

| You might've heard a price that included more than you needed, or maybe it wasn't clear what the extra $8k was gonna get you. | *While also alluding to a value issue* |
| I'm not promising it's gonna be way cheaper, but could I at least walk you through a few options so you know what's out there? | |

Once you're on a live call, you can show them that the $8k price increase produces double that in value or realize that they're super cheap and give them a bare-bones proposal to win the deal. But again, we shouldn't lock into either of those options on the cold call.

12) Situational Objection: No Resources/Bandwidth

This is similar to "call me in 6 months." People love to posture about how busy they are, but that never changes. To this day, I've never heard someone say that they have a whole bunch of bandwidth lying around.

Ask if this is a now or forever bandwidth issue (with some exaggerated humor below). Frankly, it doesn't matter. The only reason you ask is to demonstrate that you're listening and to get them talking.

Then, *use* the objection to sell the test drive where you can show them how other teams do more with less. Here's how that sounds:

Prospect: We're stretched thin and can't really can't take this on.	
You (Agree): I hear you. Literally every marketer we talk to today has 3 jobs.	
You (Incentivize): I'd hate to bug you again when you're already swamped. Mind me asking, is this just a temporary phase, or does it look like you're gonna be swamped until 2032?	*Disarmingly blunt*
Prospect: Ha ha, feels like 2030 at this point.	
You (Test Drive): I figured. Well, I'll pencil the contract start date for January 1st, 2032 for now. Look, I *know* you're swamped. But our best customers are lean teams who need some extra firepower behind them.	*Disarmingly blunt. Have fun!*

You're probably still not gonna buy this. But could I at least show you how we help other folks, just so you know what's out there?	*Mini push-away*

You're probably seeing the pattern for situational objections by now.

Let them think they've won with the objection today; convince them in the car. Later on, we'll show them the time they'll save with our product, but not on a cold call.

13) Situational Objection: Need to Hire Someone First

We get this a lot when we're selling *30 Minutes to President's Club* sponsorships. *We* know we've sold dozens of deals without a CMO in-seat because a marketing team needs to generate pipeline 365 days per year. But *they* feel like the entire world is frozen.

The problem is that recruiting searches take months. So, incentivize them to share if they've already made the hire or if the search is ongoing.

If the person starts next month, great. Send a placeholder invite for then.

If not, you can't wait. Sell them on taking a look today so they have a punch list of strategies they can present to the new boss:

Prospect: We can't take this on until we hire our new CMO.	
You (Agree): I hear you. No one wants to make a big decision that gets unwound when the new boss arrives.	*The world is frozen.*
You (Incentivize): I'd hate to bug you before they're onboard; is the search just getting started, or does the new CMO have a start date?	*Starting next month or waiting forever?*
Prospect: The search just started, so probably 1–2 quarters.	
You (Test Drive): Yeah, you're probably not gonna buy this now.	*Push-away*

But oftentimes the new CMO comes in with big ideas, and she'll wanna know what's at her disposal. So, would you be opposed to taking a look so you have a list of things in your toolkit that you can share with the new head honcho?	*Aka: look good for the new boss*

There's another iteration of this one where they're not waiting for a head honcho-type like a CMO, but they're waiting for a specialized resource to own the problem like a Head of Content. The logic still applies. Make it easy for that person to get started when they join.

14) Situational Objection: It's Not Made for XYZ

This one came up all the time when I was selling at an early-stage FinTech startup. Once we started winning the small-medium business (SMB) market, we tried to crack into enterprise accounts. But then we had to fight our own reputation of being made for the little guys.

You _really_ need to use multiple-choice here to figure out why they think they're not a fit.

From there, rely on social proof to sell the test drive. It's almost impossible for _you_ to be the person who rewrites your reputation. But if you make it seem like you're willing to put them in touch with _other_ customers, it shows you might have something worth looking at:

Prospect: It's really not made for enterprise companies.	
You (Agree): Hmm, you know, that's surprising to hear. But I can totally respect that you wouldn't even look at a tool if you weren't 100% sure it'd scale into the thousands of employees.	_Agree with the concern, not the reputation_
You (Incentivize): Look, I'd hate to have someone reach out again if we're really not a fit here. Was it something with our product, support, or something else?	_Why aren't we enterprise-ready?_
Prospect: I mostly heard in my CFO networking group that you don't scale well with public companies.	

You (Sell the Test Drive): Hmm. Look, I can tell you know your stuff, and I know I'm not gonna convince you on a cold call.	*Ego booster*
But we've had several companies go public with us, and I'd eventually be happy to make the introduction if it made sense.	*Lean into social proof hard*
But first, could I show you how we've helped other public companies so you can see it with your own eyes?	

This approach works for any product objection. Offer to show them why a respected peer chose you (dropping names works wonders if you're allowed to). Then, make the introduction to the customer reference later if it seems like a fit.

Pro Tip: Ego Boosting

Product objections often come from industry or technical experts who think they know it all. Instead of fighting their expertise, boost their ego and encourage them to see what's out there for themselves.

Existing Solution Objections Overview

Honestly, I don't eat many vegetables. My diet is largely one-dimensional: I eat all of my protein upfront, then I eat what I like.

For breakfast, I drink a protein shake. For lunch and dinner, I eat a cup of rice with a pound of ground turkey and whatever sauce makes it not taste like cardboard. Then, I often eat a pint of ice cream because I front-loaded all the boring food to make room for this.

Whenever I'd tell people about my diet, they'd usually be shocked: "That's so bad! Haven't you considered eating a more balanced diet and maybe including … *vegetables*?"

But I never listened. Why?

1. **I didn't believe them**: I'm in quite good shape, and many of these people were in worse shape than me.
2. **They didn't see my perspective**: They didn't realize that this diet accomplished the two most important things to me: hitting my protein goal and eating ice cream.
3. **I saw no problem**: What were vegetables going to solve for me?

One day, one of my gym buddies and fellow protein advocates, Noah, brought up my diet. Immediately, I thought, *Oh no … a nutrition 101 lesson from you too!?*

He actually reinforced my diet: "Honestly, man, you're in great shape. Most people can't even stick to a diet, so why change anything when yours is working for you?"

I leaned in. *Finally, someone gets it.*

No vegetables, no problem

Then he asked a question: "Curious, you're healthy. You must not get sick that often?"

I answered: "Uhh, it's been a bit more often because of the travel. Every quarter or so."

He looked over and said one word: "*Oh ...*"

I was thrown off. "What do you mean, *oh?*"

He explained: "Well, I was getting sick a lot too, then I found out that I had some pretty severe vitamin deficiencies because I was a big protein-only guy as well. So I started taking this greens powder and now I only get sick twice a year."

He concluded with … a test drive: "Wanna try a scoop of mine?"

I *dislike* vegetables (and powdered ones). But I *hate* getting sick. He knew this because I complained about it very loudly when I had to lock myself in the house for a week.

And now, I'm a damn green juice-drinking hippie.

This is what happens when prospects have a current way of doing things.

Reps make the mistake of criticizing and throwing mud at a prospect's current solution (or, in this case, my diet), which only makes them defensive and far more likely to push you away.

That said, even if they're happy with their solution, no solution is perfect. If you can get them to realize a problem on *their* terms instead of *your* terms, they might be open to a solution.

Here's how that plays out in the Miyagi Method:

1. **Agree with their current solution so they don't get defensive.** Remember, Noah first agreed with my diet and told me I was in great shape, whereas everyone else blindly told me to eat vegetables. I didn't feel the need to defend my diet.

2. **Incentivize conversation with a trap question.** Noah asked, "Curious, you're healthy. You must not get sick that often?" because he suspected this problem would exist based on my diet. The cold calling equivalent is, "It usually doesn't make sense to switch. Just so no one calls again, how do you handle [the problem]?"

3. **Sell the test drive with social proof.** Use social proof to amplify the problem. I trusted Noah's advice because he was also a

protein guy. So use the fact that *similar customers* switched over to you as proof … not your biased sales opinion.

The tone is *really* important when revealing flaws in someone's solution. Lean into the push-away. Remember, Noah started with "Curious, you're healthy" before asking the trap question. If you sound like you're asking a "gotcha" question, they're gonna get defensive.

15) Existing Solution Objection: We Do It In-House

I used to sell for a company called Carta, which provides software that helps startups manage their equity and stock option plans. In the early days, a CFO would often manage their equity out of spreadsheets—it was an annoyance, but not so annoying that they couldn't deal with it.

But, in the later stages of a company, they need to perform two accounting exercises to stay compliant: 409A Valuations and ASC 820 Expense Accounting. These are very costly and often require you to work with a third party. Fortunately, we provided both of these services.

From there, you'd simply ask a trap question to show them what was possible:

Prospect: We're good; I manage our equity myself.	
You (Agree): Oh wow! Usually when that happens, it means you've still got those spreadsheet wizard skills.	*More ego stroking*
You (Incentivize): Honestly, sounds like it's really not a pain. Just so no one else calls, out of curiosity, you must not be doing 409A valuations or ASC 820 Expense Accounting yet right?	*Trap question*
Prospect: Well, we do. But we work with Acme for that.	

You (Test Drive): *Oh* … well, the reason I ask is because most CFOs are surprised when they find out they can get those things for free because they're included for all of our software customers.	*Amplify the problem with social proof*
You'll probably keep managing this yourself, but if nothing else, could I give you a sense of what it'd look like to consolidate the spend?	*Push-away*

16) Existing Solution Objection: Competitor (Known)

Let's take another example. I sold compensation software as the VP of Sales for a company called Pave. We were 2–3x the price of our competitors because we could manage stock option bonuses that were too complex for our legacy competitors to handle.

That made for a perfect trap question:

Prospect: We're using CompEx.	
You (Agree): Oh CompEx! They're a great group. Honestly, it rarely makes sense to switch if you like them.	*Never badmouth.*
You (Incentivize): Hey, just so we don't bug ya again. That must mean you're not doing stock option bonuses, right?	*Trap question*
Prospect: Well, we are ... why?	
You (Test Drive): *Oh* ... well, other HR teams often found that managers would request bigger cash bonuses because most platforms don't let you see the value of both the cash and stock in one place. And we help with that.	*Amplify the problem with social proof.*
My guess is you won't switch, but could I give you a sense of how you might manage those things together, just so you know what's out there?	*Push-away*

Again, never badmouth a competitor. When you explain that a simi-lar customer faced a similar problem and made the choice to switch, their actions speak louder than your sales words.

But what's tricky is sometimes you can't reveal the problem … because you don't know the competitor. So you have to reveal them first. That's next.

17) Existing Solution Objection: Competitor (Unknown)

You need the name of the competitor to reveal a problem. But you can't just ask, "Who are you working with?" because prospects don't want to share their business decisions with a complete stranger.

So use multiple choice to show them that you know the most common options on the market. Then run Miyagi from the top again on that competitor.

Prospect: We're already working with another vendor.	
You (Agree): Oh, I should've assumed you had something in place.	
You (Incentivize): Just so I mark this one as dead, must be CompEx, Compensatory, or Comptastic, right?	*Multiple-choice*
Prospect: Yeah, it's CompEx.	*Got the competitor!*
Got the competitor, run Miyagi again	
You (Agree): Yeah, honestly, it rarely makes sense to switch.	
You (Incentivize): Hey, just so we don't bug ya again. That must mean you're not doing stock option bonuses, right?	*Trap question*
Prospect: Well, we are … why?	

You (Test Drive): *Oh* ... well, other HR teams often found that managers would request bigger cash bonuses because most platforms don't let you see the value of both the cash and stock in one place. And we help with that.	*Amplify the problem with social proof*
My guess is you won't switch, but could I give you a sense of how you might manage those things together, just so you know what's out there?	*Push-away*

As noted above, you'll notice we incentivize them to share more information *twice*. Try to use a different incentive for each, otherwise it comes off as canned.

18) Existing Solution Objection: Stuck in a Contract

This last one seems tricky because there's an unknown competitor *and* a timing issue, but it's exactly the same. **There's only one change**: remove the pressure of the sale *today* when you sell the test drive.

In other words, prioritize handling the competitor issue first. Then get them to take a test drive by removing the pressure of the rip and replace today:

Prospect: We're already under a 12-month contract.	
You (Agree): Oh, I should've assumed you had something in place.	
You (Incentivize): Just so I mark this one as dead, must be CompEx, Compensatory, or Comptastic, right?	*Multiple-choice*
Prospect: Yeah, it's CompEx.	*Got the competitor!*
Got the competitor, run Miyagi again	
You (Agree): Yeah, honestly, it rarely makes sense to switch.	
You (Incentivize): Hey, just so we don't bug ya again. That must mean you're not doing stock option bonuses, right?	*Trap question*
Prospect: Well, we are … why?	

You (Test Drive): *Oh* ... well, other HR teams often found that managers would request bigger cash bonuses when they can't see the value of both the cash and stock in one place. And we help with that.

Amplify the problem with social proof.

My guess is you won't switch until your contract is up, but could I give you a sense of how you might manage those things together, just so you know what's out there?

Only Change: *Push-away the rip and replace*

Once we're on the call, we can discuss our differentiators, contract buyouts, and more. But not now. They don't even want to think about a rip and replace. Get them in the car.

Now You're an Objection-Handling Machine

Whew! 18 objections. Congratulations, you officially have everything you need to open a cold call, describe the problem you solve, and handle their biggest objections to land a meeting.

Soon enough, you'll realize that objections are actually a *good thing*. And the annoying part will be when you can't even get to an objection because they don't answer or a gatekeeper is blocking your way.

That's next. Chapter 5: Gatekeepers and Voicemails.

Top 4 Actionable Takeaways from Chapter 4

- **Post-Pitch Dismissive Objections**: Reveal the real objection, then handle it.

- **Pre-Pitch Dismissive Objections:** Be disarmingly blunt; pivot back to your PBO.

- **Situational Objections**: Remove the pressure of the transition and get them in the car.

- **Existing Solution Objections**: Reveal the problem with a trap question, then sell the test drive with social proof.

CHAPTER 4 HOMEWORK:
PICK ONE OBJECTION EVERY WEEK

Can't you use a different picture, at least?

If my head is spinning from writing all that, I *know* your head is spinning trying to remember the nuances between competitor *(known)* and competitor *(unknown)*.

This is 100% normal. Do not try to cram every objection into your brain today.

Pick one objection every week and … you guessed it … practice it 30 times.

It's far more effective to master one objection at a time. Remember, you're not using a script, so you can still use *your brain* to think through the Miyagi steps for the other objections.

This is your final "Streets of San Francisco" homework.

GATEKEEPERS AND VOICEMAILS

Agenda
• How you should think about gatekeepers and voicemails
• The Gatekeeper Triple Bypass
• Double Tap Voicemails

 **B**ack in college, I worked at the USC Ticket Office. Every 20 minutes, a jolly 70-year-old alumni would call for tickets to a football game, then share unsolicited stories about the glory days from the class of 1972.

Most weeks, it was the most chill job a college kid could ask for.

But this week was different. Not a football game. Not a basketball game ...

A concert. Drake was coming to town, and I was on phone duty.

I've never answered so many calls in my life. By the end of the first day, pretty much every seat other than the nosebleeds were completely sold out.

That's when I started to miss my jolly alumni … because Drake fans didn't like that.

I answered 42 calls from teenage girls begging to get the sold-out front-row seats.

I dealt with their 42 moms who took another approach: asking (screaming) for a manager.

I turned down the 17 guys who said, "My man, hook it up for me," trying to get better seats.

And after taking this many calls from Drake's pain-in-the-ass fans, I saw it all. Schmoozers, beggars, bull-rushers—from their first few words, I knew where the call was going. And I couldn't send *every* buffoon to a manager, so I got good at maneuvering people out the door.

I got good at gatekeeping.

I picked up inbound call #301 with my gatekeeper BS sensor on high alert:

"USC Ticket Office, this is Armand. How can I help you?"

"I have tickets in section 102, row 1, under my name."

(BS. Best seats in the house. Nothing on file.)

"Sorry, miss, I don't see anything under that name. Could it have been—" She cut me off.

"He said the head of the ticket office has them. Please put me through."

(Who the heck did she think she was cutting me off? I'm the gatekeeper!)

"Sorry, miss, I have access to all the tickets in our system, and I really can't see anything. You said 'he' left tickets for you. Who are you referring to?"

"Drake. I'm his aunt."

(OOOOOOOKAY, LADY, GOOD ONE, YOU GOT ME NOW.)

I was in utter disbelief. I'd heard every ridiculous excuse for why some-one might have access to *secret* tickets, but this one topped them all. But I frankly had *no idea* what I could say to call out the BS. So, I asked this brilliant question:

"Uh. Are you sure?"

"YES, I'M SURE. WHAT KIND OF QUESTION IS THAT?"

My college career flashed before my eyes. I could imagine his tweet already:

The end of my college career (disclaimer: not an actual tweet)

I still couldn't believe it, but I put her through to the top. Worst-case scenario, I could tell my boss that I didn't want *him* to get a call from Drake himself because I stonewalled his aunt.

And I was smart for doing so. Because, yes, it *was* Drake's aunt.

Next time you call a gatekeeper, remember that I had two jobs:

Job #1 was to close the gate on strangers.

Job #2 was to <u>open</u> the gate for important people.

And your key to bypass the gatekeeper is to remind them of job #2.

You have to act like you're Drake's aunt.

How to Think About Gatekeepers

There were two reasons that I let Drake's aunt through. Reason #1 was because of what she said: she claimed to be Drake's aunt. But reason #2 was arguably more important: it was the *way* she said it. **She made me feel ridiculous for questioning her, which made it believable.**

This is how you have to approach gatekeepers. You need to make them think: *Shoot, I better get out of this person's way; otherwise, my boss is gonna be pissed.*

I know this sounds messed up, but the reality is that these gatekeepers are literally trained to detect strangers. They're bloodhounds trained to sniff out the slightest trace of pitch, a single tremble in your voice, a little telemarketer uptone … and close the gate.

And this is why the following two approaches to gatekeepers fail:

Mistake #1 is trying to befriend the gatekeeper. A gatekeeper is not your friend. Remember, by the time I got 300 calls from Drake fans, I had seen every trick in the book. I could spot the sob story a million miles away, and while I felt a bit more guilty for turning these folks down, I wasn't going to put my job at risk for a complete stranger who decided to be a bit nice on a cold call.

Mistake #2 is treating a gatekeeper like a prospect. Many sellers will reveal their product or try to convince the gatekeeper that it's worth the boss's time.

But it's standard practice for any semi-competent EA to *detect and reject* pitches … no matter how compelling they sound. When I was a VP of Sales, my EA already knew to reject *any* solicitors because she'd done it for every single executive she'd supported in her life.

You could offer the cure for world hunger, and the gatekeeper would tell you to buzz off.

Instead, we're going to walk through the gate like we own the place, and if they try to stop us, we'll give them just enough context to make them believe that we do. Here's how.

The Gatekeeper Triple Bypass

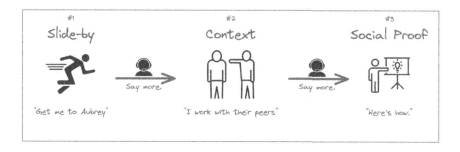

To *act* like you own the place, you need to know how someone who *actually* owns the place would act. If a guy owns a building, what does he do when he comes to visit?

He walks right in!

He doesn't timidly approach the front desk to present his ID card.

He doesn't explain the reason for his visit.

There's no need—he owns the damn place!

But if the doorman does stop him on his way to the elevator, he doesn't get thrown off and nervously explain his itinerary for his entire visit; he just says:

"I'm the owner of this building."

At which point, the doorman probably thinks: "Great, I'm fired!"

But if the doorman *still* insists on checking ID and confirming the reason for his visit, he'll comply. But only after being pressed for that information multiple times.

We're going to take a similar approach with the gatekeepers we encounter. We'll give the minimum viable information needed to get connected to our prospect. The more reasons we give for our call, the more we'll draw suspicion to the fact that we don't actually belong.

To get past the gatekeeper, we're going to take the *Triple Bypass* approach where we dose information to them, bit-by-bit and only when pressed:

You get 3 tries to bypass the gatekeeper:

1. **The Slide-by.** When they answer, ask to be put through. Nothing else.
2. **The Context**. If they stop you, share context, not product.
3. **The Social Proof**. If it happens again, lean on social proof to explain what you do.

(Disclaimer: At no point do we recommend *lying* to the gatekeeper or treating them with disrespect. There's a line between acting like you belong and explicitly lying about your identity that you should not cross. Some people recommend lying to gatekeepers. This is both unethical and likely to blow up in your face.)

Disclaimer over. Let's break it down.

1st Bypass: The Slide-by

Start with the Slide-by and ask to be put through. No company name. No small talk. Assume they will open the gate.

Tone is key here: try to sound gruff. If you're walking directly to the elevator with a stern look on your face, most doormen will think, *Yep, I'm gonna stay out of that person's way.*

Here's what you might say:

> **Gatekeeper:** Aubrey Graham's office
>
> **Nick (Slide-by):** Hey, could you get me over to Aubrey? It's Nick.

You don't state your full name when calling someone you know. Stating your full name raises the gatekeeper's suspicion and leads them to ask, "What company are you with?" or "What's this regarding?" That means your Slide-by has failed, and you now have to move to your second try.

But stating *only* your first name establishes familiarity. They'll often ask, "Nick who?" At which point, you say: "Sure—would you let him know it's Nick Cegelski?"

When you say, "Would you let him know," it sounds like the prospect *should know* it's you.

Moreover, returning their question with a question of your own reapplies the pressure on *them* to open the gate instead of on *you* to justify why you're there at all.

The one who asks the questions controls the conversation.

2nd Bypass: The Context

The sharp gatekeepers will *still* ask, "What's this regarding?" or "What company are you calling from?" after the Slide-by, so you'll have to reveal a bit more information on the 2nd bypass.

The problem is they're on high alert for anything that makes it seem like we don't belong. If you bluntly share your company name or mention your product, you'll get busted as a salesperson.

Instead, we're going to use *context* as the reason for our call to establish familiarity, just like we do in our cold call openers. For example:

- **Working with other partners.** I work with a few other Skadden partners in the LA office. Would you let him know that it's Nick Cegelski?
- **New office opening.** It's about the press release for the new office opening in Rochester. Would you let him know that it's Nick Cegelski from 30MPC?
- **Compelling event.** It's about the team's upcoming merit cycle. Would you let him know it's Armand from Pave?

Building off the 1st bypass, here's how the conversation unfolds with the 2nd bypass:

Gatekeeper: Aubrey Graham's office.

Nick (Slide-by): Hey, could you get me over to Aubrey? It's Nick.

Gatekeeper: What's this regarding?

Nick (Context): I work with a few other Skadden partners in the LA office. Would you let him know that it's Nick Cegelski?

Notice we're ending with a question that gets the gatekeeper answering our questions, not the other way around (just like we did in the Slide-by).

3rd Bypass: Social Proof

The toughest gatekeepers will push you *again* to finally reveal what you actually do, even if you nailed the Slide-by and gave them context for your call.

At this point, you have to explain what you do. But instead of using a problem proposition or a pitch, use social proof to establish yourself as a familiar face who works with their peers.

Here's how you might use social proof for a few different products:

- **Tax Planning**. We help a few other partners in the office with their tax planning: it's Northwestern Mutual. I sent him a note the other day; mind letting him know it's Nick?
- **Billing Software**. We work with a few other Buffalo firms on their client insurer billing; it's Banana Billing. I sent him a note the other day; mind letting him know it's Nick?
- **Compensation Planning Software**. We work with a few other CHROs in the Sequoia portfolio on compensation planning; it's Pave. I sent him a note the other day; mind letting him know it's Armand?

By the way, this assumes you've sent a prospecting email to them relatively recently. We'll cover that later in the chapter.

Putting it all together, here's what the Triple Bypass looks like with the final bypass:

Gatekeeper: Aubrey Graham's office.

Nick (Slide-by): Hey, could you get me over to Aubrey? It's Nick.

Gatekeeper: What's this regarding?

Nick (Context): I work with a few other Skadden partners in the LA office, would you let him know that it's Nick Cegelski?

Gatekeeper: I need to see if he's available. What company are you with?

You (Social Proof): We help a couple other partners in the office with their tax planning; it's Northwestern Mutual. I sent him a note the other day, mind letting him know it's Nick?

If you're *still* stonewalled after your 3rd try on the Triple Bypass, it's OK to throw in the towel and ask to leave a voicemail.

The unfortunate reality is that some gatekeepers cannot be passed: **Gong data shows that a gatekeeper reduces the success rate of a cold call by 39%.**

We don't recommend repeatedly fighting the impassable gatekeeper, so if you've been shut down 1–2 times, you're better off avoiding them entirely by …

- **Calling Mobile Numbers**. The gatekeeper isn't gonna answer their iPhone for them.

- **Calling During Off-Hours**. That CIO you're calling probably works longer hours than the gatekeeper. Try calling in the early morning, during the lunch hour, or after 5:00 p.m.

- **Trying a Different Channel**. The phone isn't right for every prospect; if you keep getting shut down, try another channel like email, LinkedIn, or direct mail.

Up to now in this book, we've assumed that *someone* answered the phone when we called. But the reality of cold calling is that most of the dials we make end up going to voicemail.

Before we get into *how* to leave a voicemail, the natural question is … *should you leave a voicemail in the first place?*

Should You Leave Voicemails at All?

Few topics spark more debate on a sales floor than the subject of voicemails. Let's start by looking at the case against leaving voicemails, which is quite strong:

- **Prospects never call back**. It's true. You'll *rarely* get a callback.

- **Voicemails take too much time**. It's true. You can make 25% more cold calls in the time you would've spent leaving voicemails.

- **Voicemails hurt your future connect rate**. It's true. Gong data shows that voicemails reveal you're a salesperson and reduce your connect rate on all future dials by 28%.

Every argument above holds true, but we will *still* leave voicemails. Why?

The goal of a voicemail isn't to get a callback. It's to get a reply over *email*.

Therefore, the case to leave voicemails is as follows:

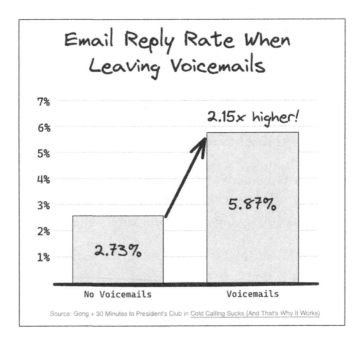

You *double* your email reply rate. Gong data shows that your email reply rate jumps from 2.73% to 5.87% for *every email you send* after leaving a voicemail.

You get to an answer faster. The reality is that some people will *never* pick up a cold call. You'll get plenty of yeses from those emails, but you'll also get quicker nos so you can move onto calling people who will actually pick up (which *saves* you time).

You can *still* maintain your connect rate by rotating your numbers. This allows you to capture the benefit of voicemails without worrying about hurting your future dials.

But we're not going to leave 100 voicemails that sound like 30-second infomercials. We're going to leave exactly two voicemails that are *designed* to double your reply rate. Here's how.

Introduction to Double Tap Voicemails

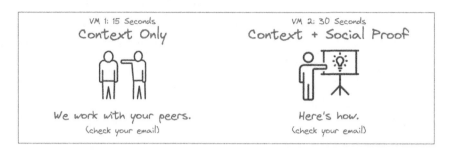

Now that you know the main goal of a voicemail is to get a reply over email, these are the main ingredients that will go into each voicemail …

Lead with context. Use context to pique their interest, then leave the pitch for the email. The moment you sell in the voicemail, they'll delete it.

Direct back to the email. Never ask them to call you back. Direct every ounce of attention to one thing: look for our email.

Keep them really, really short. No one listens to a 2-minute voicemail, and it's a waste of your time to leave anything longer than 30 seconds.

Only leave two voicemails. Your goal is to make it known that you're calling *and* emailing. Gong data shows a nice boost in overall reply rate when you leave one or two voicemails, but if you have to leave three or more, that usually means they were less likely to reply anyway.

Voicemail #	Email Reply Rate
0 Voicemails	2.73%
1 Voicemail	6.11%
2 Voicemails	5.34%
3+ Voicemails	2.20%

That brings us to our strategy: Double Tap Voicemails.

Voicemail #1: Context Only

Voicemail #2: Context + Social Proof

Sound familiar? It's just like our approach to gatekeepers.

Let's start with #1.

Voicemail #1: 15 Seconds, Context Only

Your first voicemail is going to be 15 seconds long, context only. Lead with the most important piece of context you have, then save the *entire pitch* for the email.

Here's what that sounds like:

Talk Track: Voicemail #1 (15 Seconds, Context Only)
[Context] Nick, we work with a few Skadden partners in the LA office.
[Direct to Email] No need to call back. I'm literally about to hit send on an email.

> **[Incentivize the Reply]** Just so we don't play phone tag, mind reply-ing and letting me know if it's even moderately interesting?
>
> **[Introduction]** It'll come from Armand at Northwestern, cheers.
>
>

Notice we're stacking our voicemail with what's most likely to get them to listen *first*.

- **Give upfront context** to pique the curiosity.
- **Direct to email** where they can act on it.
- **Incentivize the reply** like we did in the Miyagi Method.
- **Introduce yourself** so they can identify the email.

If you lead with your name and company, they're going to insta-delete your voicemail because you revealed that you're a telemarketer upfront. The introduction happens at the *end* for only one reason: so that they can identify our email in their inbox.

While the words are similar to those we'd share with a gatekeeper, the tone is night and day. The tone is far more familiar and friendly, similar to the Heard The Name Tossed Around Opener—leave your voicemails as if you were calling a referral.

Think: *Hey, dude! My buddy told me to give you a ring but I missed you. No need to play phone tag; I'll shoot ya a text.*

Keep an eye out for this as you listen to the voicemail talk tracks.

The context and incentive combined will get the first batch of replies. But if they still haven't replied by our next dial, we'll give 'em a bit more to draw out the reply.

Voicemail #2: 30 Seconds, Context + Social Proof

There are 3 reasons we *didn't* include anything about what we do in the first email:

1. It takes longer.
2. You can draw out a lot of responses with context only.
3. That starts to reveal that you're selling something (which, again, we want them to find out over a *live* conversation or a well-written email).

But if the context-only approach doesn't work the first time, we'll lean on social proof to explain *how* we work with their peers, but leave the details for the email. (Notice this is the exact same approach we took with gatekeepers where we only reveal more information as needed).

See the changes highlighted below:

Talk Track: Voicemail #2 (30 Seconds, Context + Social Proof)

[Context + Social Proof] Nick, we work with a few Skadden partners in the LA office … on their tax planning amongst other things.

[Direct to Email] I'm sure you've got that taken care of, but I'm about to press send on an email to give you a sense of what we're doing with those other folks.

[Incentivize the Reply] Just so we don't play phone tag, mind replying and letting me know if it's even moderately interesting?

[Introduction] It'll come from Armand at Northwestern, cheers.

Again, keep the solution for the email. The goal is to get them to sit up and think: *I don't know what they do… but they help other partners with this stupid tax problem, so let me at least look at the email to see what's going on.*

At this point, you're probably wondering … *What in the world are we saying in this email that's going to get them to reply?*

Let's take a brief intermission to share how your cold *emails* should tie to your cold *calls*.

How Should My Emails Tie to My Cold Calls?

Let's take a step back. It's rare that you would only make one cold call or send one email to a prospect. It's best practice to use a sequence of 10-14 prospecting touchpoints that includes cold calls, cold emails, and LinkedIn touches over 30 days.

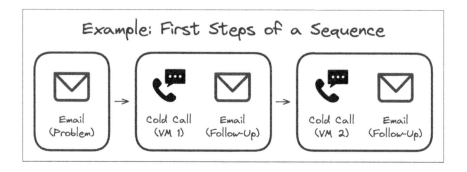

Focusing on calls and emails, the first few steps in the sequence usually look like this:

- Day 1—Email
- Day 3—Call + Follow-up Email
- Day 5—Call + Follow-up Email

The first email often includes everything you'd cover in the first 60 seconds of a call. The context, triggering problem, one-sentence solution, and interest-based call-to-action.

Subject: Sequoia <> Acme <> Pave

Hey Jane, noticed your team was backed by Sequoia.

When you're leading HR at a fast-growing Sequoia-backed company, it often drives you crazy to see employees ask for *another* raise when the value of their equity just tripled.

So, we've built total rewards statements for other Sequoia portfolio companies so their employees can see the value of their equity, cash, and benefits in one place (and realize life's not so bad).

Open to taking a look?

Example 1st email from my Pave days (Compensation Software)

If they don't reply after you send this first email, use voicemails and short follow-up emails to draw attention *back* to this email instead of pitching over and over again.

Pro Tip: Pull Up Your First Email While You're Dialing

This email often contains all of the context you need to open a cold call or leave a voicemail. Pull it up as you dial each prospect if you want an easy way to access your research (this often means you don't even have to have your research spreadsheet or CRM notes open).

That means a few days after the first email, you leave a voicemail and immediately send a follow-up email like this:

Subject: Re: Sequoia <> Acme <> Pave
Hey Jane, just left you a voicemail.
Any thoughts?

Example 2nd email (reply to same thread)

Explicitly reference the fact that you left a voicemail to create the connection between the calls and the emails.

Yeah, it's short. But this email often gets just as many replies as the first.

3rd email? Do it again, but give 'em just a bit more with social proof.

Subject: Re: Re: Sequoia <> Acme <> Pave
Hey Jane, tried you over the phone again.
Here's a <u>case study</u> I thought might be helpful for more context.
Mind letting me know if this isn't a fit?

Example 3rd email (reply to same thread)

It's the same approach that we took with gatekeepers and voicemails. Slowly give more information to draw out a reply as needed—a case study, a short demo video, etc.

To recap this very brief email lesson …

Put your "pitch" in the first email and use the next two voicemails and emails to draw attention back to it.

There are a million other cold *email* tactics that we aren't going to cover in this book on cold *calling*. That said, below you'll find a (free) example outbound sequence with example messaging templates so you can see how the calls, emails, and LinkedIn touches work together over 30 days.

Template: Armand's 30-Day Outbound Sequence

What's Next?

Guess what ... you've made it to the end of *both* Sections 1 and 2.

- You know how to win the first 60 seconds with openers and problem propositions.
- You know how to overcome any objection like Mr. Miyagi.
- You know how to Triple Bypass gatekeepers and leave Double Tap voicemails.

That means you literally have every single thing you need to navigate a cold call.

By now, you're at *least* 2x better than the average rep *on* the phone.

But the secret to being 4x better lies in what you do *off* the phone.

Welcome to the third and final section of *Cold Calling Sucks (And That's Why It Works)*.

How to be a machine.

Top 4 Actionable Takeaways from Chapter 5

- **Act Like You're Drake's Aunt**. The gatekeeper doesn't need to hear your pitch. They don't need to be your friend. Walk in like you own the place.

- **The Gatekeeper Triple Bypass**. Slowly share information, starting with the slide-by, then the context for your call, and then social proof to frame what you do.

- **Double Tap Voicemails.** Voicemail 1 is context only; voicemail 2 adds the problem.

- **Tie Emails to Calls**. Send one tailored problem email upfront, then use your two voicemails and follow-up emails to drive back to it.

CHAPTER 5 HOMEWORK:
DOUBLE TAP VOICEMAIL SCRIPT

Write down your Double Tap voicemail script and get this thing on autopilot. Most of the voicemail is static, and you really shouldn't have to tailor them beyond the context you share upfront.

Practice it so many times that you waste no words. The first voicemail should *really* be under 15 seconds, and the second voicemail should *really* be under 30 seconds.

Here's another beautiful gift for you … a table!

Voicemail 1: **Context Only**	[Context] [Direct to Email] [Incentivize the Reply] [Introduction]
Voicemail 2: **Context and Problem**	[Context + Social Proof] [Direct to Email] [Incentivize the Reply] [Introduction]

A Small Request to Close Section 2: An Honest Review

If you've made it this far, that probably means you're booking meetings by now.

For an entire year, we spent 4 hours every single day beating the living daylights out of each other to make this the best cold calling book you've ever read. We wrote, re-wrote, re-drew, and re-voiced over every chapter more times than you can imagine.

Writing a book is far from the most profitable content channel. But we believe it's the most powerful to make the biggest impact for the most sellers. And from day 1, we've always prioritized the audience experience over selling out for a quick buck.

So it'd mean the world if you took two seconds to give us an honest review on Amazon. It's the easiest thing you can do to spread the word and help us get this in the hands of more sellers. We'll read every single one.

Review *Cold Calling Sucks (And That's Why It Works)*

HOW TO BE A MACHINE

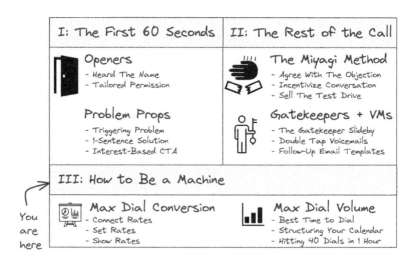

I: The First 60 Seconds	II: The Rest of the Call
Openers - Heard The Name - Tailored Permission	**The Miyagi Method** - Agree With The Objection - Incentivize Conversation - Sell The Test Drive
Problem Props - Triggering Problem - 1-Sentence Solution - Interest-Based CTA	**Gatekeepers + VMs** - The Gatekeeper Slideby - Double Tap Voicemails - Follow-Up Email Templates

III: How to Be a Machine	
Max Dial Conversion - Connect Rates - Set Rates - Show Rates	**Max Dial Volume** - Best Time to Dial - Structuring Your Calendar - Hitting 40 Dials in 1 Hour

You are here

Let's pretend that you were the *best* cold caller in the world.

How could you book more meetings if you weren't allowed to work more hours?

Well, let's go through the list:

1. ~~Get really good on the phones.~~ (Nope, you're already the best).
2. Call a list so good that other reps think your territory is unfair.
3. Make more cold calls in less time.

The secret to becoming a cold calling machine lies in #2 and #3.

If you call the prospects who are most likely to pick up and have the problem you solve ... you'll book *2x the meetings* without making more cold calls!

And then, if you learn to make more cold calls in less time ... you'll book *4x the meetings*.

Section 3 teaches you to break the cold calling math equation *off* the phone.

Chapter 6 covers how to maximize your dial conversion. Double your connect rates, set rates, and show rates *without* making more cold calls. It's possible.

Chapter 7 covers how to maximize your dial volume. We'll show you how to fit 40 dials in one hour every single day, even when your calendar is twice as full as the next rep's.

Get ready. It's time to become a cold calling machine.

HOW TO MAXIMIZE YOUR DIAL CONVERSION

Agenda
• How to maximize your connect rates
• How to maximize your set rates
• How to maximize your show rates

 **"K**enny's Weekly Activity: 400 dials. 0 meetings booked."

The hardest-working rep on my team was in last place on the leaderboard.

He was making more dials than anyone else. He was crushing the role-plays. Nothing was adding up.

So I sat down with Kenny's manager and asked him two questions:

1. How many *conversations* did he have? (*Not:* How many cold calls?)

2. Who did he have those conversations *with*?

We started with the 1st question. On 400 cold calls, Kenny had a mere 10 conversations (a 2.5% connect rate, last on the team).

We combed through all of his dials that *didn't* connect:

- Bad corporate line
- Same bad corporate line dialed 3x for different prospects
- Busy number dialed for the 2nd time
- Busy number dialed for the 3rd time

Kenny wasn't tracking any of his bad numbers, which meant he was hitting the same brick walls over and over again.

We ran the same exercise on the 10 dials that *did* connect:

- Company with 10 employees (way too early for us)
- Company we literally lost a deal with last week
- Great company! (But he called the wrong department)
- Great company! (But he called a lowly analyst)

I didn't even have to listen to the calls.

Kenny could've made 4,000 more dials and wouldn't have booked a single meeting because he was calling bad numbers, bad companies, and the wrong people.

And while this was a particularly extreme case ...

I've coached over 100 SDRs in my career and found that the #1 rep is *never* #1 on the activity board.

Why? Because they put in the work *off* the phones to drastically increase their results *on* the phones:

- They have *double the conversations* by calling the prospects most likely to pick up.

- They *book double the meetings* by targeting the prospects most likely to buy.
- They *keep all the meetings* by making sure those prospects actually show up.

Don't get me wrong, they still dial a *lot* and they're really good on the phones.

But they get more juice from 200 dials than most reps get from 400 dials.

How to Get More Juice Out of Fewer Cold Calls

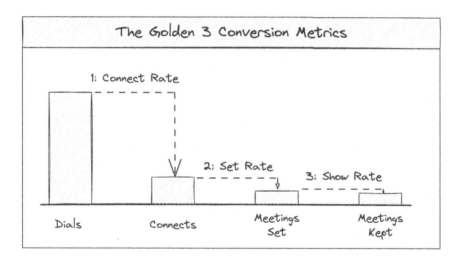

It's not voodoo magic. You can make a few small tweaks that drastically impact your results and take way less time than making an extra 50 dials.

The Golden 3 Conversion Metrics dictate the number of meetings you keep when you make 100 cold calls:

1. **Connect Rate.** What % of your prospects picked up the phone?
2. **Set Rate.** What % of those conversations turned into meetings?
3. **Show Rates.** What % of those meetings actually show up?

Using Gong data, here's what the Golden 3 Conversion Metrics look like for an average rep vs a top quartile rep:

	Average Rep	Top Quartile Rep
Connect Rate	5.4%	13.3% (2.5x better)
Set Rate	4.6%	16.7% (3.6x better)
Show Rate	56.9%	72.5% (1.3x better)

How big of a difference does this actually make?

Let's assume two sellers have the *same* dial volume of 200 dials per week for 4 weeks.

The only thing we'll change is their Golden 3 Conversion Metrics.

	Avg Rep	Top Rep	Difference
# Dials	800	800	**Unchanged**
# Connects	43	106	**2.5x the conversations**
# Meetings Set	2	18	**9.0x the meetings set**
# Meetings Kept	1	13	**13x the meetings kept**

On the same number of dials, the top quartile seller gets <u>13x the results</u>.

The difference between the average reps and the top reps is *massive*.

The beauty is that the average rep is horrendous at cold calling, and you're already way, way past that by picking up this book in the first place, let alone making it this far.

If you can even pull *one* of the remaining levers above, you'll massively increase the results on *every single dial* you make.

Let's start with the one that determines how many conversations you even get to have.

Four Ways to Maximize Your Connect Rate

Mobile + Direct Lines	Mark Your Tracks (1, 3, 4917)
Law of Diminishing Returns	Prevent Spam Tag

It's pretty demoralizing to call 40 people and have 0 conversations. Leaving voicemails for an hour straight is neither effective nor fun.

To maximize your connect rate, there are four places to focus:

1. Prioritize mobile and direct lines.
2. Mark your tracks.
3. Abide by the law of diminishing returns.
4. Prevent yourself from getting spam-tagged.

Let's break them down one by one.

Prioritize mobile and direct lines whenever possible since these numbers have a higher connect rate and allow you to skip gatekeepers and phone trees. It's generally accepted to call mobile phones in the US, and for every one prospect who gets upset you called their cell, you'll have twenty others who only answered *because* you called their cell.

Mark your tracks. Your first set of calls through a new list of numbers should be the last time you sit through a long phone tree or call a screeching fax machine.

As you dial, mark the quality of each number as red, yellow, or green so you remember which ones are good or bad.

Blank = Unconfirmed	It rings 4+ times, but it's a generic voicemail, so you're not sure it's them yet.
Green = Confirmed	You're 100% sure it's the right person. Rings multiple times and their VM greeting confirms it's them. These are the numbers to call!
Yellow = Not Sure	Smells fishy. Ex: Busy lines or one-ring-straight-to-voicemail. If it happens again on the next dial, move it to Bad.
Red = Bad	Repeated busy lines, fax lines, wrong numbers. Once you've marked a number as red, never waste a dial on it again.

From here, leave yourself notes for any obstacles you encounter:

- **Phone Trees.** Write down the numbers you used to navigate phone trees so you can just punch in (6, 2, 4716) without having to listen to the phone tree all over again.

- **Corporate Lines**. Document dead-end corporate lines at the company level so you don't redial them for every prospect.
- **Front Desk**. Same as above. Avoid over-dialing the front desk in a single dial blitz. It gets awkward when you ask them to connect you to 4 people back-to-back.
- **Gatekeepers**. Even if you can't pass them the first time, you'll be far more prepared to bypass them the next time.

If you're using a sales engagement platform that allows you to "tag" numbers as bad, you can bulk skip *all* of those tasks before you start dialing so that you're constantly pruning your list.

Abide by the law of diminishing returns. I'm sure you've heard legends about the dogged salesperson who finally booked a meeting with their dream prospect after calling them every single week for a decade straight.

The reality is that they would've booked far more meetings if they made those extra dials on prospects who would've picked up before dial number 506.

Draw your lines of diminishing returns ahead of time so you know when it's time to move on to the next prospect.

- **5 dials in 4 weeks**. When you've literally cold called someone every week for a month straight, give them a rest for a month and try cold calling other prospects for now.
- **Stop after two voicemails**. Per the last chapter, two voicemails are enough to reap the benefits of increasing your email replies. Don't waste time leaving a 3rd.
- **Avoid impassable gatekeepers.** If they keep shutting you down, avoid them by calling your prospect's cell, contacting them on other channels, or dialing off-hours.

Prevent yourself from getting spam-tagged. Armand recently posted on LinkedIn that he doesn't get cold called much. ~~To his dismay~~ It brought him tremendous joy that this led to 5 people cold calling him in a 24-hour timeframe.

The problem is, literally 4 out of 5 numbers were marked as spam by his cell provider.

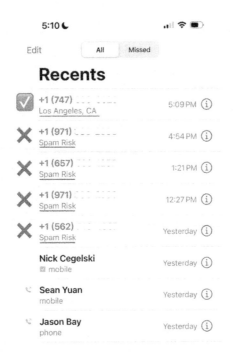

Exhibit A: Armand getting what he asked for.

Here are some things you can do to prevent yourself from getting marked as spam:

- **Register your phone number.** Wireless carriers reference call registries to determine your phone number's reputation. You can register as a non-spam caller with those registries here: https://freecallerregistry.com/fcr/.

- **Rotate your phone numbers.** Wireless carriers monitor unusual spikes in call volumes[7], so many sales engagement platforms and VOIP providers let you buy and rotate additional lines to call from so that you don't tarnish your number.

- **Test your number regularly.** Many purchased numbers are recycled, so call your personal line from any new number first to confirm that it's not *already marked as spam*.

- **Call during business hours.** The FTC considers business hours between 8 a.m. and 9 p.m.[8], so an 8 a.m. or 5 p.m. block is fine to pass the gatekeeper. A 5 a.m. or 10 p.m. block is not.

- **Don't repeatedly call bad numbers.** Carriers will flag you[9] if you repeatedly call bad numbers (yet another reason to document your tracks).

Before we wrap on connect rates, there are some frankly unethical approaches that some folks use to try to boost their connect rates.

Avoid tactics like double or triple dialing someone to make them think you're an emergency from a loved one, using *67 to hide your phone number or cold FaceTime (this one's sort of a joke, but people actually do it).

These might get your prospect to answer the phone, but the second they realize you tricked them into taking a sales call, you'll be lit up by a pissed-off prospect who's going to report you as spam and never want to do business with you.

---

[7] https://www.voicespamfeedback.com/vsf/bestPractices
[8] https://www.ftc.gov/business-guidance/resources/complying-telemarketing-sales-rule
[9] https://www.voicespamfeedback.com/vsf/bestPractices

2. How to Maximize Your Meeting Set Rate

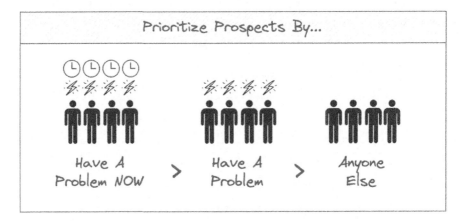

You can make the best hot chocolate in the *world* ... but you're not gonna sell many cups of cocoa in the Sahara Desert.

The #1 way to increase your set rate is to call people who actually have the problem that you solve (crazy, I know).

In order of priority, the prospects who are most likely to book meetings are the ones who ...

1. Have a problem *now*
2. Have a problem
3. Anyone else in your ideal customer profile

The higher they are on the list, the more you should call them.

The way you build this list is in *reverse* order. Start with a big list, cut all the junk out of it, then prioritize the best prospects that remain.

Let's walk through how you do this in practice.

Step 1—Pull a List of Qualified Companies (Or People If You're in B2C)

Build a list of all the reasons you *shouldn't* work an account and disqualify the junk first.

For example, I was selling compensation software, and we literally *couldn't* sell to any companies with the following traits:

- Non-US based
- Under 100 employees
- Non-tech

You should be able to identify bad accounts within the first 30 seconds of picking them up (The 30-Second Rule) so that you can spend your research time on the accounts that'll actually buy.

Step 2—Tier Your Accounts A/B/C

From here, research and tier the remaining companies. Build a list of the top 5 things that make a company likely to buy, prioritizing the *timing-based* signals at the top.

This varies *greatly* by company, so be sure to build your own list. For example, my top 5 research triggers at Pave looked like this:

- Have an upcoming compensation review (Problem *now!*)
- Fundraised within the last 3 months (Problem *now!*)
- Hiring a compensation person (Problem *now!*)
- Growing over 10% per year (Problem)
- References "generous equity compensation" in job postings (Problem)

From here, I tier accounts as follows:

> **A Tier**—have a problem *now*.
>
> **B Tier**—have a problem.
>
> **C Tier**—anyone else who fits my ideal customer profile.

A*dd two extra dials* to your A and B tier accounts because they are far more likely to convert to a meeting if you get them on the phone.

Step 3—Call the Right People on the Accounts

Don't be the rep that wastes an A tier account by working only one person. If you decide to work an account, work the *entire* account. That usually means (continuing the Pave example):

- *All* "above the line" executives—VP/Chief HR Officer and VP/ Chief Financial Officer
- *All* "at the line" department leads/champions—Head of/Director of HR Operations, Compensation, or Total Rewards
- *Some* "below the line" business users—Manager of People Operations, Compensation, or Total Rewards

(P.S. While pulling these contacts, you may consider doing extra "person-level" research for your A tier accounts in this step. For instance, if I could find something on the Head of Compensation's LinkedIn about running merit cycles, I'd always add that to my notes here.)

Reps spend way too much time calling *junior prospects* or *wrong departments*. A lowly HR analyst might take a meeting, but they rarely have any influence on a purchase.

Don't be afraid to call high into an account. You'd be surprised that the best way to get the old-school executives on the line is often through a good old cold call since their inbox is well-guarded by an EA.

Step 4—Prioritize Your Dials (Within Reason)

If they want to buy <u>now</u>, call them!

Don't be the rep who cherry picks their dials. If you stack your A and B tiers with more dials, your list will naturally contain more dials on the better accounts.

That said, there are a few *intent signals* that are worth prioritizing atop your dial blitz:

- If someone opens your prospecting email 5x … call them first!
- If someone visits your pricing page … call them first!
- If someone replies over email with an objection … call them first!
- If someone has a *new* compelling event (i.e., raised a round) … call them first!

You can set up notifications for most of these signals in either your sales engagement platform, a marketing automation platform, or a research database.

Start with those high-intent dials, then call the rest of your list top to bottom.

*   *   *

To hammer this home, I had one rep who *refused* to make more than 50 cold calls per week.

But he booked 3 meetings per week off those dials because he was so damn good at scavenging for hidden gold in the CRM.

You don't even have to be *that good* on the phones or make 400 dials per week to have success when you're calling people who *actually* have the problem you solve.

Now, it's just a matter of getting those people to show up.

3. How to Maximize Your Show Rate

Gong provided data on whether or not you should send a confirmation email and, if so, how many emails to send. It was actually quite inconclusive.

That said, we believe that a *good* confirmation email is better than no confirmation email because it allows you to build goodwill and prevent a no-show.

Our practical answer is to send day-before confirmations for same-week meetings.

In your email, don't ask if the meeting is on. *Assume* it's on, and include something that shows you've taken the time to prepare. Here's an example:

Example Day-Before Confirmation Email
Hey Jane, looking forward to our chat tomorrow.
By the way, saw that you all announced the new hydraulic potato peeler—excited to hear more live.

This reveals that there's a human on the other line who's preparing for the call and reduces the chance of a no-show.

For a meeting **2+ weeks out, send** *both* **a day-before and a week-before confirmation.** Your first email can be the exact same one as the above, and your second email can be a simple reply (looking forward to tomorrow).

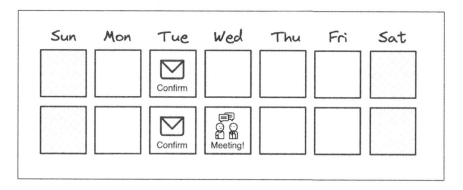

From there, if the meeting begins and they haven't shown up, follow this cadence:

- Email them at the 2-minute mark ("We're on! Putting the Zoom here at your fingertips").
- Call them at the 5-minute mark.
- Call them again at the 8-minute mark (the only time when it's acceptable to double dial).

Then, if they actually no-show, never delete the invite. Move it 3-4 days out, then send backup times over email (using a touch of guilt in your message):

Example No-Show Email
Hey Jane, bummed that we missed you earlier.
We take time to prepare for all of our calls, and we were looking forward to our chat.
I moved the invite a few days out, mind letting me know if that one works or if these other ones below are better? (include backup times)

I know it's tedious to send the confirmations and chase down the no-shows. But I promise it's far easier to keep a meeting than it is to find a new one.

Putting It All Together: Your Golden 3 Cheat Sheet

Putting it all together, here's your Golden 3 Cheat Sheet, including benchmarks for each metric and ways to improve them:

	Average	Top Quartile	How to Improve It
Connect Rate	5.4%	13.3%	- Prioritize mobile and direct lines - Document your tracks - Abide by the law of diminishing returns - Avoid getting spam-tagged
Set Rate	4.6%	16.7%	- Master your phone skills - Call the right companies - Call the right people - Call at the right moment
Show Rate	56.9%	72.5%	- Send 1-2 confirmation emails - Email and call during the no-show - Punt the invite after the no-show

Now that you know how to eliminate junk dials and squeeze the juice out of every cold call … we can *responsibly* teach you to ramp up your dial volume like a true cold calling machine without sacrificing quality.

This final chapter of *Cold Calling Sucks (And That's Why It Works)* is your cold calling Red Bull.

Top 4 Actionable Takeaways from Chapter 6

- **Connect Rate**: Never call bad data twice, document phone trees, avoid spam behavior

- **Meeting Set Rate**: Purge disqualifiers, prioritize the top companies, and call high.

- **Show Rate:** Used 1-2 personalized confirmation emails to build goodwill.

- **No Shows:** Never delete the meeting invite. Punt it and suggest times.

CHAPTER 6 HOMEWORK:
YOUR NO CRAPPY DIALS PUNCH LIST

Use the table below to build your own 4-step research punch list, then run your account list from top to bottom.

If you know exactly what to look for *before* you start your account research, you'll be able to tear through most accounts in under 5 minutes without getting distracted by every random detail on the website.

Step 1: Account Disqualifiers	1. 2. 3.
Step 2: Top 5 Buying Signals	1. 2. 3. 4. 5.
Step 3: People to Contact	Above the Line: At the Line: Below the Line:
Step 4: Intent Signals	1. 2. 3.

Preface to Dial Volume: Should You Use a Dialer Technology?

Whenever we talk about making more cold calls, sellers ask if they should use a *parallel dialer*, which allows you to call multiple people simultaneously.

This allows you to make far more calls and connect with more prospects in less time. Some even allow you to "drop" prerecorded voicemails for further time savings.

The major drawback with parallel dialers is that you have no idea who's going to pick up. That means leading with context in your opener is nearly impossible (unless you get really good at reading the research that pops up in the dialer as quickly as humanly possible). So you need to rely on less effective, generic openers like the untailored permission-based opener.

Furthermore, these systems have a slight lag when the prospect picks up, which creates an awkward pause that gives the prospect "call center vibes" from the start.

So our recommendation is as follows:

- **If you have a massive territory**, a slight % decrease in call conversion doesn't matter as much if you're connecting with 3x the prospects and have a big pool to rotate through.
- **If you have a small territory (i.e., enterprise sales)**, every call connect *really* matters, so you might want to dial them one by one.

Since these tools aren't ubiquitous (yet), we wrote the next chapter assuming you're not using one. But even if you are, the next chapter will *still* help you make more calls in less time.

HOW TO MAKE MORE COLD CALLS IN LESS TIME

Agenda
• The *perfect* time to cold call
• How to make time for prospecting even when you have a full pipeline
• How to double your dials in the same 60-minute cold calling session

"**Y**ou're not allowed to pee until you've made 10 cold calls."

Every morning before work, I'd chug a Venti iced cold brew and embark on a 45-minute commute to the office. I'd walk into work bursting at the seams and do what any normal human being would do: use the restroom, *then* start working.

I'd wander over to my desk, boot up my computer, and start clearing out my email inbox. I'd see my fellow salespeople across the floor get sucked into the mundane discussions of what they watched on Netflix that weekend. And sometimes, I'd get pulled in too.

I *knew* I'd have to make some cold calls eventually, but I thought that starting out with some admin tasks and office banter would "warm me up" to make my cold calls.

The issue is that the exact opposite would happen.

Every second that passed, the phone would look heavier and heavier and other non-revenue-generating activities would look more and more appealing.

Next thing you know, it'd be 11 a.m., and I'd have 0 cold calls and 0 meetings on the board.

But things changed when, a month into my sales career, I read a quote that changed my perspective:

> **"You don't need to feel good to get started, but you do need to get started to feel good."**

I realized that the first cold call of the day is always the hardest one to make. I never felt like picking up the phone at 9:03 in the morning ... and I definitely felt like it even less at 10:03 or 4:03.

But once I'd knocked out my first couple of dials for the day, it wasn't so hard to keep the momentum going and rip the rest of them too. I'd get into a flow state of opening the next dial task, punching my 7 digits, and skimming my call research while the phone was already ringing.

Getting started was the hard part. And I wasn't doing myself any favors by wallowing in a state of anxious procrastination for the entire morning by checking email, over-researching prospects, or talking about TV shows I had no desire to watch.

My solution was the 10 Dial No Pee Rule. No peeing allowed until after I'd broken the seal (pun intended) on my first 10 cold calls for the day.

The next day, I burst into the office fueled by my Venti cold brew. But instead of hitting the restroom, I immediately opened up my laptop, *remarkably* motivated to hit my first 10 dials so that I could relieve my aching bladder.

From there, finishing up the rest of my cold calls (after a brief bathroom break) was easy because I was already riding the wave of positive momentum from the first 10. By the top of the hour, I'd have 40 cold calls done before anyone else had even picked up the phone.

Moving forward, I never used the restroom until I made my first 10 dials.

Full bladder = full pipeline.

The Perfect Time to Cold Call Is When You'll Actually Do It

When you force yourself to make your calls before you're allowed to do anything else, you're guaranteed to get them done every single day.

Conquering the hardest thing you have to do kicks off a *virtuous cycle* that makes the rest of your day seem easy by comparison. Nothing feels better than knocking 40 dials down and booking 3 meetings by 10 a.m. when the rest of the world hasn't even started. From there, you'll be primed to tackle more and more revenue-generating activities to extend your lead.

But when you start with the *easiest* admin tasks in the morning, you get into a *vicious cycle* of momentum, and your day starts running *you*. You get caught in the mindless inertia of task clearing and inbox checking, and the idea of cold calling feels worse and worse every second.

By noon, it's too late. The whole world is awake. An active deal blows up your inbox, a demo goes off the rails, your boss calls a surprise forecast, or an emergency comes up with the kids.

"I'm not a morning person" is no excuse here. *No one* feels like making cold calls at 9 a.m., 12 p.m., 4 p.m., or *ever*! Remember, you don't have to feel good to get started, but you do need to get started to feel good.

Every year, a new study comes out about the best time of day to cold call. That leads to a whole bunch of other excuses that sound like: "I read online that it's best to dial on Thursdays between 3 and 4 p.m., but I have a prospect meeting then, so I won't dial today."

Consistency **of effort matters far more than micro-optimizations created by timing your dials.** One missed dial blitz sets you back 40 cold calls. A measly 5% increase in connect rate from timing your calls means jack if it occasionally causes you to miss a call block and thus lose 20% of your dials for the week.

And guess what? Gong data shows that the best time to call *is* in the morning anyway!

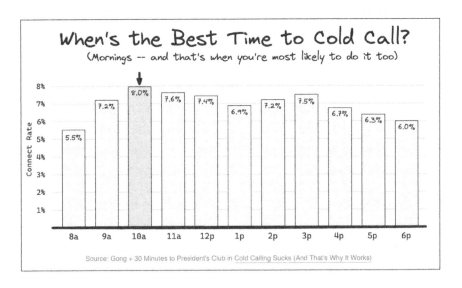

So now that there's *really* no excuse ... do it for 4 weeks in a row, and you'll become addicted to the positive morning momentum and never go back. I promise.

The Calendar of a Cold Calling Machine

 Sticking to your morning dials is easier said than done. You need to structure your entire calendar in a way that ensures you have time to prospect in the morning *and* do the rest of your sales job.

There are two things required to do that effectively.

1. **Front-loading**: Do the hardest revenue-generating activities before anything else (that means cold calling).

2. **Time Blocking**: Dedicate time blocks for those activities where you're *only* allowed to do that one thing. If you're in a dial block, you're not doing *anything* other than dialing (that means you *close* your inbox).

Starting with front-loading, I prefer to divide my day into thirds as follows:

- **Green Hours (8 a.m.–12 p.m.)**: Hit your daily prospecting goal in the morning when you're most likely to do it while allowing customer meetings to fill in the gaps.

- **Yellow Hours (12–3 p.m.)**: Take *most* customer meetings in the afternoon, then use any remaining slots to get *ahead* on prospecting or mix in some afternoon dials.

- **Red Hours (3–6 p.m.)**: Defer *all* of your administrative tasks to the end of the day or dedicated inbox time blocks.

If you're not color coding your calendar yet, this is an easy way to start. Code your prospecting activities green, customer calls yellow, and admin activities red.

Over time, add more colors for different meeting types (1st calls vs. 2nd calls, recurring meetings vs. one-offs), but start simple before you try to turn your calendar into a bag of Skittles.

Now that we have our general calendar buckets, let's build an ideal sales calendar in 4 steps, starting with the single biggest culprit of distractions: your inbox.

Step 1—Confine Your Inbox to 8:30 a.m., 12:00 p.m., and 3:00 p.m.

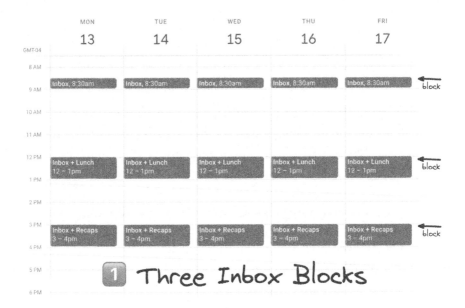

Many sellers think that staring at their inbox all day and having a 2-minute email response time means they're going to close deals faster. They claim that they *have* to send the proposal now. They don't have time to prospect because they're "closing deals."

This kicks off the mediocre middle rep tailspin. They get completely consumed by every deal in their pipeline until it closes, then realize that they don't have another one and have to start *all over again*. The pipeline roller coaster begins: hit quota, miss quota, hit quota, miss quota.

The reality is that customers are on back-to-back calls just like you, and half the time, they're not even going to reply until they clear their inbox at the end of the day anyway.

Tame your inbox (and internal chat) to 3 windows at 8:30 a.m., 12 p.m., and 3 p.m. These 3 windows create peace of mind when you're prospecting. You *know* you'll be able to check your inbox every 3 hours. That means you can close it *entirely* in the gaps in between (no notifications, no phone checking, nothing).

The recap can wait. The proposal can wait. Unless you're in the middle of an *urgent* contract negotiation or literally sending it for signature … it can *all* wait.

If you're relying on checking your inbox on the toilet to drive your deals, that means your deals are driving *you*.

Step 2—Set Two Prospecting Blocks in the Morning and One in the Afternoon

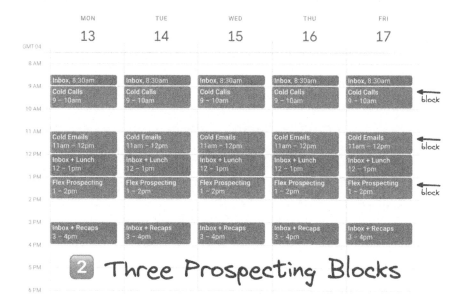

Now that you're not having a heart palpitation wondering if a prospect sent you an email, it's time to get your prospecting done *first*. As a full-cycle seller, set 3 prospecting blocks:

- **One hour for cold calling at 9 a.m.** Always do your cold calling *first* because it's the hardest prospecting activity, otherwise you'll be far more likely to skip it later in the day.
- **One hour for cold emails at 10 a.m. or 11 a.m.** Depending on when your customer calls land, send your cold emails as your next task in the morning.
- **One hour for flex prospecting at 1 p.m.** Use the final block to get ahead, make some extra afternoon dials, or handle any left-over prospecting.

Try to hit your prospecting goal *before* 12 p.m., then use the afternoon to get ahead. Those first two blocks get you to quota. The third block gets you to President's Club.

If you're an SDR, BDR, or meeting setter who doesn't take customer meetings, you essentially do 1.5–2x the prospecting in the hours by:

- Adding an **extra dial block** in the late morning (Green Hours).
- Adding an **extra email block** in the early afternoon (Yellow Hours).
- Adding an **extra 1–2 hours of research time** to build up your dial inventory in the late afternoon (Red Hours).

For all of the full-cycle sellers (and aspiring ones), let's talk about customer calls next.

Step 3—Take Customer Calls in the Afternoon or Morning Gaps

Once you start booking meetings, suggest times in the afternoon to keep your Green Hours as green as possible. Cold calls feel awfully heavy at 2 p.m., but taking a meeting with a customer (who isn't trying to hang up on you) tends to sap much less energy.

That said, I get it. The reality is that some prospects will only be available in the morning. Make an exception for these and schedule *some* customer meetings in the morning.

But here's the rule:

You're not allowed to delete that dial block or move it outside of the Green Hours.

If you have to schedule a prospect meeting over a morning dial block, immediately move that dial block to another morning slot within the

Green Hours. This will prevent you from letting this exception slip into a habit of overbooking customer calls in the morning.

Step 4—Move All Administrative Tasks to the End of the Day

4   Admin at END of day

What's left? All of the administrative tasks that *happen* to occur within the world of sales but aren't *really* the revenue-generating activities.

We've already confined the inbox, so move the rest of the distractions to the end of the day.

- **Internal Meetings.** Ask your manager to schedule your 1:1s at the end of the day (I get it, you can't move *all* team meetings, but you can at least start with this).

- **Deal Correspondence.** At 3 p.m., write *all* of your recap emails back-to-back (take good notes during the meeting), make your CRM updates, and prep for tomorrow's calls.

- **Research and List Building**. Do all of your list building in the final two hours of the day so that you can come in ready to prospect the next morning.

The last one is especially key. There's nothing that'll prevent you from making your cold calls more than *not knowing who you're going to cold call*.

That means you need to do *all* of the following things the night before your dial blitz. Otherwise, you will be *unable* to make 40 cold calls first thing in the morning.

- You need to pull a list of accounts (companies in B2B, people in B2C).
- You need to research those accounts, including the people to call.
- You need to find contact information for those people.
- You need at least 60 of them to yield 40 dials when accounting for bad numbers.

You've got your 60-dial tasks locked and loaded. You've got your dials blocked in the morning. The only thing left? Make sure that you hit *all* 40 in that hour.

But first … I *know* there are still some skeptics here who don't think they can make the time to cold call. So, I have a loving note for you first.

A Loving Note to My Full-Cycle Reps Who "Can't Dial Every Day"

When I'm giving this training to teams, this is usually when I get the *most* complaints from middle performers who can't fathom the idea of sending a recap email at the end of the day or prioritizing prospecting over responding to customers.

Again, you've made it this far. So I don't believe that this is you.

But just to prove that I'd never ask you to do something that I wouldn't do, I'm going to share two examples where I've eaten my own dog food.

Example 1) As an AE, I did 267% of quota while consistently making 200 dials per week and made a bet with my manager that if I didn't, I would eat nothing but Greek yogurt for an entire day.

I'm lactose intolerant, and I can assure you I never missed this commitment.

But frankly, the next example was the one that pushed me to my limit.

Example 2) I led Pave from $100K to $13M+ in revenue in two years as their VP of Sales. But I joined early on as the 9th employee when there was literally *no team to lead*.

So I started as a player-coach. That meant I carried a quota as a seller *while* I built out the team as the leader, which included:

- Setting up all the systems infrastructure
- Hiring the entire team
- Training the entire team
- Managing the entire team
- Finding product-market fit
- Running the board meetings
- *AND* running the podcast, webinars, and newsletter for *30 Minutes to President's Club* on the side

But I wanted to demonstrate street cred to both my CEO and to my team.

So every single morning, I cold called for an hour in front of the entire 10-person company to show them that there is *always* time for prospecting.

Screenshot from my favorite sales ops guy at Pave (thanks, Luis!)

If I can work 3 jobs and find one hour to make cold calls every day, you can do it too.

Rant over. Let's talk about how to make the most of that hour.

How to Make 40 Dials in an Hour Without Sacrificing Quality

When I was an AE, I'd invite my team to join me in my morning cold calls every day at 9 a.m.

Many reps would struggle to put up more than 20 dials, but one rep in particular struggled the most. This is what morning sessions with "5-Dial Dave" looked like …

9:00: We start dialing.

9:05: Dave rolls in.

9:06: "How's it going so far, guys?"

9:10: "Okay, let's see who's gonna get a good old fashioned 'cold call' today …"

9:13: "These 10 look good, lemme make sure I get my research ready …"

9:19: "Quick lil' inbox check just to make sure I don't miss one of my two deals."

9:24: "Okay, okay, we're ready. It's dial time, guys."

Approximately 12 cold calls later, almost certainly upon first rejection

9:45: "Well, look at how time flies, gotta get ready for my 10 a.m. Closing deals!"

When people complain that cold calling takes too long and instead decide to mass-blast 3,000 emails to a utility company in the Mojave Desert, their dial blitzes look like this.

The average seller lets everything from the smallest inbox ping to account research prevent them from attacking the hard task that's good for them: cold calling. So let me be clear …

If you cannot hit 40 cold calls in an hour, you are probably spending most of your dial blitzes screwing around instead of cold calling.

And no, this does not mean you're spam dialing or neglecting research (you did that the night before for a reason).

Here are the **5 ground rules** to make 40 dials in an hour without sacrificing on quality:

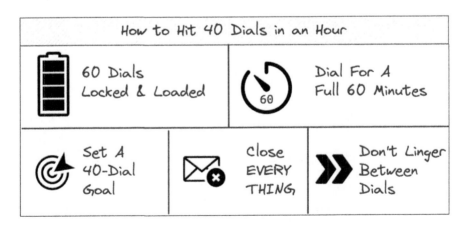

How to Hit 40 Dials in an Hour		
60 Dials Locked & Loaded	Dial For A Full 60 Minutes	
Set A 40-Dial Goal	Close EVERY THING	Don't Linger Between Dials

1. **60 dial tasks locked and loaded**. Again, all research should be done the night *before*. Have your research sheet/CRM ready on one screen while you dial on the other. As you punch in numbers on one side, pull up your prospect research on the other so you can still make well-personalized dials.

2. **Dial for a full 60 minutes**. *Never* schedule a 30-minute dial blitz. Your first 5 dials are your worst 5 dials. If you've ever had a prospect pick up on the very first cold call, it's like waking up and having your spouse sneeze in your mouth. When you commit to an hour, you commit to pushing through the warm-up dials as you gain momentum.

3. **Set a 40-dial goal**. I used to commit to 40 dials in an hour, which is about as fast as I could personally push it without cutting conversations short or rushing through dials.

4. **Close *everything* else**. No email, no chat, *no other browser windows* open. Literally put your phone on do-not-disturb so you block out notifications entirely. Do not multitask as you dial (other than pulling up your research). This will only elongate your dial blitzes and put you at risk of getting caught flatfooted.

5. **Don't linger between dials**. Finish a dial? Punch in the next. Book a meeting? Send the calendar invite, and move on to the next. Take a hard rejection? I know it hurts ... but you *have* to pick up the phone again. You don't have to feel good to get started, but you do have to get started to feel good. Each no gets you closer to a yes.

Every single high-performing rep I've ever coached has been able to hit 40 dials in an hour. You've made it this far into the book, so I know you can do it too.

So ... How Many Dials Should I Make in a Week?

I'm going to give you the mathematical answer first, then the practical answer.

First, figure out how many dials it takes you to *keep* one meeting. Use *your* metrics to work your way backward. Using the top quartile Golden 3 metrics as an example:

What It Takes to Keep One Meeting	#	Notes
Meetings kept	1.0	Our goal
Meetings set	1.4	72.5% show rate
Connects	10	16.7% set rate
# Dials to keep one meeting	**62**	**13.3% connect rate**

From there, figure out how many meetings you need to hit quota. If you're an SDR, this is easy because you often have a meeting-based quota. If you're a full-cycle seller, it gets a bit more complicated. Here's an example using big round numbers:

Monthly Goal	Amount	Notes
Revenue Goal	$100,000	This is your monthly quota
Pipeline Goal	$400,000	25% win ratio
Opportunity Goal	10	$40,000 average deal size
Meeting Goal	20	50% meeting-to-opportunity ratio
Meetings Goal (From Dials)	10	Assumes you get 10 meetings from inbound/other prospecting channels
Monthly Dial Goal	620	62 dials per meeting
Weekly Dial Goal	**155**	**4 weeks in a month**

Yeah, complicated. And you probably don't even have access to half of these numbers, which is why I recommend you take the practical answer.

Practical Answer: I've coached hundreds of AEs and SDRs and tried to run this math an obscene number of times. Somehow it *always* ends up coming back to 1–2 hours of cold calling per day with the exception of people who are calling into a super-focused list of enterprise accounts.

So put a stake in the ground and start with the following:

- Full cycle sellers should dial for 1 hour per day (150–200 dials per week).
- Meeting setters (i.e., SDRs) should dial for 2 hours per day (300–400 dials per week).

From here, increase your weekly dial load if you need more meetings to hit quota.

But *don't* lower it. Why?

Sure, you *might* be able to hit your quota off 4 days of dialing.

You *could* take a day off.

But the next day, that phone will look just a *little* bit heavier.

That bad day turns into a bad week.

Next thing you know, you're on the roller coaster with every other middle-performing rep.

Hit. Miss. Hit. Miss. Hit. Miss.

The moment things get busy, *most reps* convince themselves that it's okay to miss a day of dials, and that's exactly when the pipeline roller-coaster ride begins.

But I know *you're* not most reps.

Wanna know how I know?

Because you're approaching the end of this book.

*   *   *

This is your final recap and homework assignment.

The only thing that could possibly stop you now is ... *not* picking up the phone.

But don't worry about that because if you have *any* final hesitations ...

We've got you covered in the conclusion, "How to Kill Call Reluctance Forever."

Top 4 Actionable Takeaways from Chapter 7

- **Hit your cold calls first thing in the morning** to conquer the most taxing, most important revenue-generating activity *first*.

- **Divide your day into Green, Yellow, and Red Hours** for prospecting, customer calls, and admin work with 3 dedicated inbox blocks in between.

- **Make 40 dials in an hour** by preparing your research ahead of time, removing all distractions, and maintaining momentum in between dials.

- **Dial for 1–2 hours every single day** to avoid the pipeline roller coaster.

CHAPTER 7 HOMEWORK:
COMMITMENTS AND CONSEQUENCES

When I was selling insurance, I used to miss my dial commitment every other week. My coach was so upset with me that she literally canceled our 1:1s and said I had to earn them back by hitting my dial commitment 4 weeks in a row.

So, in front of the entire floor, I put a $100 bill on the table and said, "Don't give it back to me until I hit this for 4 weeks straight."

I hit it for 4 weeks and never missed it again.

This led to me raising the stakes with "The Greek Yogurt Challenge" and bringing the "Commitments and Consequences" board to every sales team I've ever run.

Your challenge is to share your weekly dial commitment with someone and agree to a consequence if you miss it.

Consequences I've seen in the past are:

- **The NASCAR SDR.** Only make left turns in the office for an entire day.
- **The Mustache.** You must wear a fake mustache at all times (except on customer calls).
- **Greek Yogurt.** Eat nothing but Greek yogurt for a day (this was mine).
- **$100 to an enemy.** Donate $100 to a cause that you *disagree* with.

You must start with the stick until you respond to carrots.

HOW TO KILL CALL RELUCTANCE FOREVER

This question always comes up when we teach cold calling:

"How do I overcome my cold call reluctance?"

You break into a cold sweat before you pick up the phone.

You nervously multitask to avoid the first dial.

You *hope* the CEO doesn't answer to avoid the confrontation.

You end the dial blitz early after landing one meeting while you can escape unscathed.

You take a rejection so bad that you look around to make sure no one heard it.

I don't call these feelings out to attack reps struggling with call reluctance.

I call them out because I've personally felt every single one of them too.

In this closing note, I'd like to share what helped me overcome my call reluctance to prevent you from taking the *only* certain path to failure: *Never picking up the phone.*

The Key to Killing Call Reluctance

Call reluctance is fundamentally a confidence issue.

I define "confidence" as the extent to which you believe your inputs will lead to the outputs.

In other words, do you believe that you will book a meeting if you make enough cold calls?

You can try to "manufacture" this confidence by …

- Reading 100 more books so that you *think* you're prepared.
- Writing out scripts for days until you *think* you've covered every objection.
- Researching prospects so long that you *think* you know everything about their business.
- Ritualizing with positive self-talk to make yourself *think* you'll book a meeting.

But the only way to *really* prove it to yourself is to make it a reality.

You need to make so many cold calls that you become numb to the rejection, and your mind makes the connection that 50 dials = 1 meeting over time.

1st time you hear the prospect implode? You freak out.

100th time you hear the prospect implode? You laugh.

Why? Because you *know* the meeting is coming because you've seen it happen 100 times.

*   *   *

Am I suggesting you go into the game underprepared? Absolutely not.

You need two things to get started.

1. You need to know your minimum viable talk tracks.
2. You need to say them out loud or role-play them 50 times.

And by making it to the end of this book ... you've already done both of those things.

So, you sign a contract with yourself to do the inputs *until* the outputs become a reality.

- You make the calls *before* you do anything else.
- You make the calls *every single day* as part of your routine.
- You set a goal for the week and a *consequence* if you miss it.

There is no more deciding whether or not it is a good day to dial.

This is the contract that no one else is willing to sign.

This is the contract that becomes your ticket to President's Club.

Cold Calling Sucks, and That's Why It Works

 This book ends right where it began. There's no getting around the suck of cold calling.

No matter how good you get, you'll still deal with rude prospects, stonewalling gatekeepers, and countless voicemails in search of the handful of prospects who'll agree to meet with you.

The average sellers forget that their success in sales is determined by the number of uncomfortable conversations they're willing to seek out. The discomfort and monotony of cold calling erodes their commitment—until they allow themselves to make excuses like:

- I called 20 people and only one answered. There's gotta be an easier way.
- It's more effective nowadays to send uber-personalized emails instead of calling.
- It's almost the end of the quarter. I gotta focus on closing.
- Mondays aren't good for calling because prospects are in meetings.
- Fridays aren't good for calling because prospects are gearing up for the weekend.
- Today's super busy. I'll just make twice as many tomorrow.

The sellers who make President's Club face the same "suck" of cold calling as everyone else. The only difference is that they don't allow it to stop them from making the calls.

Why? Because they know that's when the average rep quits.

In many ways, cold calling reminds Armand and me of the hardest practices we had in our college wrestling days. Olympic Gold Medalist and the greatest wrestling coach of all time, Dan Gable, famously said the following:

> *When I'd get tired and want to stop, I'd wonder what my opponent was doing. I'd wonder if he was still working out. I'd try to visualize him. When I could see him still working, I'd start pushing myself. When I could see him in the shower, I'd push myself harder.*

You cannot beat average performance if you don't do things differently than the average performers. The suck becomes your *advantage* because it causes your competition to drop out when things get hard.

When the calls start to suck, that's exactly when you get ahead of the pack.

Picking up this book was your first step. Now, you have everything you need to succeed on the phones.

Your final step is to pick up the phone and start dialing your way to President's Club.

The cold calls are going to suck, but hey, that's why they work.

ONE FINAL ASK

For the last 12 months, Nick and I have followed this schedule:

1. Wake up.
2. Write this book for 4 hours.
3. Do everything else it takes to run *30 Minutes to President's Club*.

Every day, we beat the heck out of each other to make every page worthy of your most valuable asset in sales—your time.

As of the completion of this book, our website still has this line that we wrote when we started the podcast in 2020:

> *Throw your 400-page sales book in the trash and start landing deals today. Zero theory, no-nonsense. We cut through the BS and get to the point so you can spend more time learning new skills that make a difference today.*

If you feel this book held true to the promise above, it'd mean the world if you wrote us a review on Amazon.

It takes two minutes, and we read every single one.

Review *Cold Calling Sucks (And That's Why It Works)* on Amazon

---

YOUR TICKET TO PRESIDENT'S CLUB

I f you want more content like this book, our newsletter is the best place to start.

Every week, we pick one sales topic and break it down in the most actionable newsletter in sales.

That could mean ...

- How to write the perfect cold email
- How to open a cold call
- How to uncover pain on a sales call
- How to end a negotiation in one cut
- How to scale a sales team from 1 to 100 reps

We include highlights from our most popular podcast episodes, scripts & templates, and more—so you'll know exactly which next steps to take.

Step 1 was mastering the phones to fill up your calendar.

Step 2 is mastering everything else to make it to President's Club.

Subscribe to the 30MPC Newsletter

Scan the QR code or go to 30mpc.com/newsletter to subscribe.